"Clear, focused, full of action-oriented suggestions. This is THE new management reference guide!!"

— ANDREA NIERENBERG, AUTHOR OF
Nonstop Networking, NEW YORK, NY

"Doug delivers concise, effective advice to his clients. Now, anyone who wants to accomplish more in today's 24/7 world can learn how to do so from a true expert in the art of business productivity."

— NATHAN DERBY, MANAGER OF EDUCATION AND DEVELOPMENT,
HARVARD MANAGEMENT COMPANY, CAMBRIDGE, MA

"The techniques in this book definitely made me more efficient and profitable. I was good at what I do. Now I'm even better!"

— SCOTT HENDRICKSON, NATIONAL ADVERTISING DIRECTOR,
Sports Illustrated for Kids & *Sports Illustrated for Teens*, NEW YORK, NY

"Pam's facilitation work with our Board and physician's group was exquisitely powerful, helping us navigate through a difficult transition as a cohesive team. Get this book if you want to live a more enjoyable life with much less stress."

— ALLEN KORNEFF, PRESIDENT & CEO,
DOWNEY REGIONAL MEDICAL CENTER, DOWNEY, CA

"At last, a book that brings time management into the 21st Century. This book is contemporary, practical, and well researched. A priceless guide to smarter, better business and living."

— ALASTAIR RYLATT, AUTHOR OF
Winning the Knowledge Game, SYDNEY, AUSTRALIA

"This book hits the nail on the head. Doug and Pam clearly spell out the foundations of success and take people exactly where they need to go. I highly recommend it!"

— MICHAEL J. BRATHWAITE, EXECUTIVE DIRECTOR,
BUSINESS NETWORK INTERNATIONAL FOR NEW YORK CITY, NY

The 25 Best Time Management Tools & Techniques

How To Get More Done Without Driving Yourself Crazy

Pamela Dodd
&
Doug Sundheim

Published by:
Peak Performance Press, Inc.
Ann Arbor, MI

First printing, August 2005
Second printing, January 2007
Third printing, September 2007
Fourth printing, September 2008

Acknowledgments

Much of this book was built "on the road" in the course of running our consulting business. We learned firsthand what works and doesn't work in managing our own time. We also learned that you can't accomplish much without support from others.

We'd both like to thank Michele DeFilippo, 1106 Design, for squiring this book through the publishing process. She was a gem to work with and made book publishing seem easy.

We'd also like to acknowledge the following friends, family, and colleagues:

Pam — Kudos to my Internet marketing colleagues. Thanks to Jim Edwards and Joe Vitale for starting me on the book path. Many thanks to Yanik Silver for the time spent on the phone with me. Special thanks to Ken McCarthy and System Club members Elsom Eldgridge, Susie and Otto Collins, and Bettina Mueller. And deep appreciation to Brad Fallon, Andy Jenkins, and StomperNet members. Both learning communities par excellence!

I'm also grateful for the interest and encouragement of friends Barry Grieder, Larry Witzleben, Diane DiCarlo, and Melissa Personette. I deeply appreciate the financial generosity of my mother, Peg Hurlbut.

Most of all, I want to acknowledge two important men in my life. Many thanks to my husband, Tom Connellan, for his love and considerable help during this project. A published author himself, he gave me space to do things my own way. I'm also grateful for the strong business and personal relationship I have with my co-author, who is also my son. No parent could ask for a more loving, creative connection.

Doug — I want to thank several people who helped shape this book, including Mike Van Cleave, Maria Boafo, Nathan Derby, Nancy Donohue, Alex Toia, and Armando Meija.

Many others have encouraged me along the way. I'd like to thank Bill Markel for showing me what's possible with dogged determination. I'd like to thank Debra Sparks being one of my biggest fans. Thanks also to Jason

Bonadio for offering a good ear and sound advice when I needed it. And thanks to my dad, Jim Sundheim, who hasn't always been sure where I'm headed but hopes like heck that I get there.

Finally I'd like to acknowledge two special women in my life. My wife, Daryn Morgenstein, was a great help as we put these ideas together. And thanks to my mom for a lifetime of support and conversations. In so many ways I wouldn't be where I am now without her.

Table of Contents

INTRODUCTION

We all want to be more productive. We also want to have more fun and enjoy life more. These goals aren't mutually exclusive. It all boils down to time and how you use it.

Before we tell you a little about this guide, let's be clear on a few basics. First, fundamental facts about time:

- Everyone gets exactly 24-hours a day. No more. No less.

- Time can't be owned, borrowed, or saved.

Time is a convenient concept invented to mark our days more precisely than morning, noon, and night. In ancient times it was measured with shadow sticks and sundials. Now we use clocks. Regardless of device, time can't be managed. It passes. That's it.

What we're really managing when we talk about time management is the *events* of our lives, including the tangible and intangible stuff connected to these events. For convention's sake, however, we'll call it time management like everyone else.

Second, you are at the center of how time occurs for you. Contrary to popular belief, time management doesn't change things "out there." It changes you and your relationship to things "out there." Successful people know this and use it to their advantage. So can you.

The benefits of good time management are considerable. People who manage their time well:

- Get more done

- Feel less stress

- Have better relationships

- Feel better about themselves and their lives

- Have ample time to do the things they like to do
You can have all that too. It's up to you.

What makes this guide different from other time management books is its breadth and brevity. It covers the whole range of time management topics in a short, to-the-point fashion.

We've loaded the guide with the best available information on time management. Our strategy for finding this information was simple. We read the Amazon.com customer reviews for over 40 time management books. Then we bought and read the top 20.

A word about Amazon reviews. We realize that authors' friends and family often write many of the favorable reviews. However, no books worth their salt can survive solely on cronyism. Luckily folks who don't like books write reviews too. Plus we formed our own opinions.

The structure of this guide came from the commonalities we identified in the 20 books we read. The 25 Best Tools and Techniques fall into five related areas:

- Section I (Focus) shows the best ways to find out what's really important to you.

- Section II (Plan) explains the best ways to manage your plans for results.

- Section III (Organize) describes the best ways to manage your living and work spaces.

- Section IV (Take Action) discusses the best ways to manage your actions.

- Section V (Learn) covers the best ways to continually improve.

How you use the guide is up to you. Read it from start to finish or zero in on specific areas. Since no time management system is right for everyone, we've included many options. If one solution doesn't work, try another. Do something. Anything. If you just read, you won't manage time any better than you do now.

Remember, changing a lifetime of habits takes time, sometimes as long as a year or two. Be patient with your efforts to manage yourself better. Your ultimate reward is the life you've always wanted to live.

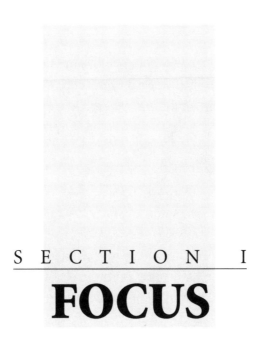

SECTION I
FOCUS

MANAGING YOUR TIME BETTER does **not** start with jumping immediately into action. You've probably done that already. Shooting from the hip might work in the short-run, but it isn't an effective long-run strategy.

People who manage time well and maximize their productivity focus on what's important to them, on what they really want. In this section we discuss four ways to help you determine what **you** really want:

- Put It in Writing

- Find Out What Time Means to You

- Identify Your Values

- Create a Vision

We can use an analogy of building a house to explain why these four elements are key to managing your time well:

- Putting things in writing organizes the project. Without written records and plans, construction would be a disaster.

- Finding out what time means puts a monetary worth on it. How can you maximize your investment in your house?

– Values describe the type of home you're building. City, suburbs, or country? Traditional, modern, or contemporary? Big, medium-sized, or small? One story, two or more? Three bedrooms or four?

– Vision is the blueprint of the house. It describes exactly what your house will look like when it's done.

In Section II — Plan, you'll learn how to set goals and create an action plan. Using the house analogy, your goals and action plan are the specifications. They answer questions such as: What materials will you use? Who will do the work? In what order will it be done? By when?

Focusing is the basis for everything else. Skip this step and you've missed the rock-bottom foundation of good time management.

NUMBER

1

Put It In Writing

IT'S IMPOSSIBLE TO CARRY EVERYTHING around in your head. Something always gets lost.

Time management experts and top executives recommend writing down what's important to you — your values, vision, goals, projects, appointments, lists, people to contact, etc.

Capturing your thoughts on paper (or electronically) frees up your creative energy. You don't have to worry about forgetting anything. You feel completely free to focus on what's important.

Note: If your primary mode of processing information is auditory, you might try dictating your thoughts first. These days recording and speech recognition technology is reliable and can quickly convert audio to digital text.

We cover the best ways to store your thoughts and ideas in Tool #5 — Use a Personal Planning System. Jump to that chapter if you want a system to use as you complete the exercises in this section. If you'd rather keep on reading, writing your notes in this guide or in a notebook is fine for now.

NOTES:

2

Find Out What
Time Means To You

IF YOU WANT TO MANAGE YOUR TIME BETTER, you need to know what time means to you. You've always had a relationship to time, even if you aren't aware of it.

Below are two ways to find out how you use time and what it's worth to you.

KEEP A TIME LOG

Many time management experts believe a time log is very helpful in revealing how you're using your time.

Note: A time log isn't necessary for improving your time management, although it can open your eyes to where your time *really* goes (not where you *think* it goes). You'd be surprised!

How to keep a time log:

1. For seven consecutive days, keep track of **everything** you do from when you wake up to when you go to sleep. Record your activities every 5 minutes (Alec Mackenzie, *The Time Trap*, recommends every time you shift your attention). Be very specific.

2. Record everything, including socializing, daydreaming, fantasizing, and interruptions. Log your time as you go, not all at the end of the day.

3. At the end of a week, total up how you spent your time (e.g., meetings, 7 hours; working on project X, 5 hours; sleeping, 40 hours; playing computer games, 14 hours; watching TV, 20 hours; brushing teeth, 42 minutes, etc.).

4. Analyzing your log, answer these questions:

   – How much time did you spend on important things? On routine tasks? On time wasters?

   – When were you most productive?

   – When were you least productive?

   – When and what were your worst interruptions?

   – Did you use travel and waiting time productively?

   – To what extent did you achieve your main goals each day?

   – What did you do that you shouldn't have been doing?

Wolfe Rinke (*Don't Oil the Squeaky Wheel*) suggests asking these questions to analyze your time expenditures at work:

- "What would happen if I didn't do this task or activity at all?" If nothing will happen, stop doing it. If you don't know what would happen, trace its origin to find out why it was required in the first place. If you can't find its origin, stop doing it and monitor what happens. You can always reinstate it if necessary.

- "Will this activity move me closer to achieving my top three priorities?" If not, stop doing it (unless your boss requested it; then go on to the next question).

- "Can this be delegated?" If so, delegate it. If not, learn how to do it more efficiently and effectively yourself.

ESTIMATE YOUR TIME WORTH

Dan Kennedy (*No B.S. Time Management for Entrepreneurs*) offers this eye-opening exercise.

Many time management experts calculate the value of a person's time based on an eight-hour workday. Kennedy correctly points out that none of us is productive eight hours a day.

He figures on average we're productive one out of every three hours and instead uses the *productive (or billable) hour*. See how his five-step formula changes the equation:

1. Determine your base earnings target for the next calendar year. (If you don't have a base earnings target, make one up, even if it's a bit flaky.)

2. Divide it by the number of annual workday hours (e.g., 220 days × 8 = 1,760 hours).

3. Multiply what you got by 3 (or whatever your time productivity vs. nonproductivity multiple is).

4. The answer is your time value *per hour*.

5. Divide by 60 to get your time value *per minute*.

The fact that your time is worth much more than you think should have a big impact on how you use it.

Kennedy offers this advice for living up to the value of your time:

- Post your time value where you can see it often.

- Hang out with the people who respect and value your time. Drop those who don't.

- Delegate or eliminate those tasks below your time value.

Now that you know how you've been using your time and what it's worth to you, you can begin to make room for more congruence in your life. The more congruence you have between where you are and where you want to be, the happier and more fulfilled you'll be. Identifying your values is the best way to start on that journey.

NUMBER

3

Identify
Your Values

Values are worthwhile or desirable qualities, standards, or principles.

WHEN YOU'RE CLEAR ABOUT YOUR VALUES, LIFE FLOWS. You're pulled toward what makes you happy and productive. You feel satisfied and fulfilled.

When you're unclear about your values — or espouse values that other people think are important — life is a struggle. Circumstances push you, often in directions you wouldn't necessarily choose. You feel frustrated, anxious, and ineffective.

Life shifts from *push* to *pull* when you identify, own, and begin living from your own values. Your experience of time also shifts.

The exercises in this chapter will help you identify, sort through, and prioritize your values.

Note: While these exercises will give you a good ballpark sense of your values, identifying your values usually takes a while to gel. Be straight with yourself as you do this work and take the time you need.

There are a number of ways to find your values. We offer the two most popular — Value Stories and Value Checklist.

VALUE STORIES

Your values are embedded in the stories you tell about yourself. Follow directions for the four scenarios below. Completing at least two scenarios is a good idea.

- Pick one scenario to write or dictate about.

- Tell your story quickly, without editing or analyzing.

- Give as much detail as possible.

- Go back and identify the values, stated or implied, that you see or hear in your story.

- If it would be more helpful, tell your story to a friend who can take notes and reflect your story back to you with the implied values.

SCENARIOS

1. Talk about something you do very well (e.g., a skill inside or outside work). Say why you do it so well and what feels right about it. Speculate about what makes this particular skill such a success for you.

2. Describe an accomplishment at any age that left you feeling deeply fulfilled or satisfied.

3. What values do you feel you must honor or part of you dies?

4. What would you be doing if time and money weren't concerns?

VALUE CHECKLIST

The most common way to identify values is by checking off one-word descriptors on a list. However, when one word doesn't express the essence of what you value, you may need to create a value string.

Value strings are two or three words or phrases that describe a significant space or area for you. For example:

- Beauty/Harmony

- Integrity/Walk the Talk

- Leadership/Empowerment/Collaboration

It takes longer to identify values this way, but it's time well spent if it describes what's important to you better.

Begin the values checklist exercise on the next page.

1. Check all the values you think apply to you.

____ Acceptance	____ Excitement	____ Moderation
____ Accountability	____ Fairness	____ Money
____ Achievement	____ Faith	____ Nature
____ Adventure	____ Family	____ Openness
____ Affection	____ Flexibility	____ Order
____ Authenticity	____ Forgiveness	____ Partnership
____ Balance	____ Freedom	____ Passion
____ Beauty	____ Friendship	____ Patience
____ Belonging	____ Fun	____ Peace of Mind
____ Camaraderie	____ Generosity	____ Perseverance
____ Care	____ Genuineness	____ Play
____ Challenge	____ Gratitude	____ Pleasure
____ Collaboration	____ Growth	____ Prestige
____ Commitment	____ Happiness	____ Quality
____ Compassion	____ Harmony	____ Recognition
____ Competence	____ Health	____ Reflection
____ Competition	____ Honesty	____ Respect
____ Confidence	____ Honor	____ Responsibility
____ Contribution	____ Humility	____ Security
____ Cooperation	____ Humor	____ Serenity
____ Courage	____ Independence	____ Service
____ Creativity	____ Influence	____ Sincerity
____ Curiosity	____ Inspiration	____ Spirituality
____ Decisiveness	____ Integrity	____ Stability
____ Development	____ Intuition	____ Status
____ Devotion	____ Involvement	____ Success
____ Discipline	____ Joy	____ Teamwork
____ Effectiveness	____ Kindness	____ Tolerance
____ Efficiency	____ Knowledge	____ Tradition
____ Empathy	____ Leadership	____ Trust
____ Empowerment	____ Learning	____ Variety
____ Excellence	____ Love	____ Wealth
____ Enthusiasm	____ Loyalty	____ Wisdom

2. Choose up to 10 values from those you checked. Include values not on the list plus values from your Value Stories.

   If some of your values seem to go together, create value strings. Try different combinations to see what fits best.

3. List your top 10 values in any order.

4. Now reduce your values to no more than 6. Aim for brevity and clarity. Some of your values are more fundamental than others. See what can be collapsed or combined. Once you have 6, prioritize them (Top value = #1).

5. Write this list on an index card or sticky. Put it where you can read it daily.

6. Keep revising the list until you can honestly say, "Yes. This is me!"

7. Write your final prioritized list (fewer than 6 is fine). Put it where you can read it often (preferably in your personal organizer).

Reviewing and revising your values is covered in Technique #22 – Review & Reflect. The next step is to create your vision.

NOTES:

NUMBER

4

Create
A Vision

Vision is a statement of how you want to live your life.

SOME PEOPLE USE THE TERMS "vision," "life purpose," and "mission" interchangeably. Others think they mean different things. There's no consensus. We'll use vision; you can call it what you like.

Your vision is your unique blueprint for effective time management and a more fulfilling life. It uses your values to paint a clear picture of what you say you stand for. An empowering vision:

- Shows how you choose to spend your time and energy.

- Reflects what you're passionate about; it has heart.

- Motivates you to reach beyond your past performance to accomplish even bigger things.

- Acts like a compass, pointing you in the right direction.

- Provides you (and others) with continuous inspiration.

Can you live your values without a vision? Perhaps. But your efforts are more likely to be hit or miss. Without a clear statement about how your values play out in your life, you're prone to drift, distraction, and allowing circumstances to run your life.

Below we give you two ways to craft your vision. Whichever you choose, set aside uninterrupted time to do this work. Like the values exercises, it takes time to create a compelling vision.

Note: We don't give examples of vision statements because we don't want to bias your efforts. You can read examples in Stephen Covey's books (*The 7 Habits of Highly Effective People* or *First Things First*).

Also, Author Jim Collins (*Built to Last, Good to Great*) offers great points about vision in a December 30, 2003 article in *USA Today*.

Collins says your vision should fall at the intersection of your answers to these questions:

- What are you deeply passionate about?

- What activities do you feel just "made to do"?

- What can you make a living at?

If more than 50% of what you're doing falls outside these three areas, you need to stop doing what doesn't contribute. Don't settle for good enough.

Here are two ways to construct a vision:

WRITTEN VISION STATEMENT

1. For each of your values, write down your answer to this question — "If I'm living from this value, what am I doing?" Be specific. Describe what's going on in your life and how things sound, feel, and look.

2. Make your statements both *inspirational* and *realistic.*

3. Use the *present tense,* as if you're living your values now.

4. Make sure what you write reflects *all* your values and that it covers all aspects of your life — work, family, relationships, leisure, spirituality, etc.

5. Distill your writing into one or more sentences for each value. You can stop there or combine it in a meaningful way.

6. Your statement can be any length, as little as a few words to as much as three pages. The shorter, the easier to remember. But don't skimp on what's important to you.

7. Keep writing, reading, and revising until you can say without reservation, "Yes. This statement is my vision for my life."

ARTISTIC VISION STATEMENT

1. Use music, poetry, and/or art to express your vision.

2. Share it with others so they get what it means to you.

Once you're satisfied with your vision, keep it nearby, preferably in your personal planning system (you can use pictures if it's a work of art). Review it regularly.

Keep in mind that your vision is not a To-Do to be crossed off a list and forgotten once it's done. It's a living document (or work of art). Treat it with reverence and respect. It's your bedrock of being.

In Technique #6 — Set Goals, we show you how to plan for concrete actions that bring your vision to life.

NOTES:

S E C T I O N   I I

PLAN

MOST OF US DON'T PLAN WELL. As a result, we don't know how to leverage our time. The most common reasons people give for not planning are:

– No time to plan

– Already know what to do

– Think planning doesn't work

– Don't like To-Do lists

– Don't know how to plan

These are nothing but convenient excuses for avoiding responsibility for your own success.

All time management experts believe planning is key. You need a map to show you how to get from where you are to where you want to go. Without a map, you're likely to get sidetracked, stalled, or stuck. Good intentions are never enough.

How you plan is a good indicator of your relationship to results. If you've been getting disappointing results, here's your chance to learn how to plan better. In this section we give you four ways to organize your plans for results:

- Use a Personal Planning System

- Set Goals

- Plan Backward

- Prioritize

In Section III — Organize, we'll cover organizing your material and digital stuff.

5

Use A Personal Planning System

ALL TIME MANAGEMENT EXPERTS recommend using a personal planning system. It serves as your main productivity tool.

Some people swear by electronic planners. Others prefer paper planners — commercial organizers, small notebooks, steno or legal pads, or index cards. It doesn't matter what you use as long as you use it consistently and it helps you be more organized and productive.

- If you have a system that's already working well, great! Skim this section for practical pointers.

- If your system isn't serving you, figure out why. You may need to find something else.

- If you don't have a system, you need to get one.

We cover paper and electronic planners below. If you prefer something else, determine what you need and make it work.

PAPER PLANNERS

The look, feel, and functionality of your system are important. You'll save considerable time, money, and frustration if you do your homework upfront.

Visit online stores to get a sense of what's available. Look at styles, formats, and prices. You can pay more than $200 for planners with fancy leather covers. However, inexpensive planners are fine.

If you decide to buy something new, don't invest in all the bells and whistles until you've got a system that works.

No matter what you spend, choose *a calendar layout* and *cover closure* that suit your typical schedule and work style.

The format of your planner calendar is especially important. It will greatly affect your productivity. The one- and two-page-per-day formats give you plenty of room to schedule and make lists, but you can get lost in the details. If your days aren't filled with appointments and things to do, using these formats is probably a waste of space (and money). Many time management experts prefer weekly calendars so you can better see how you're using your time.

Be aware of the different look and feel of calendars, especially if you use more than one kind. For example, most wall calendars start on Sunday. Most weekly planners start on Monday. This difference could have you entering information on the wrong day or giving someone the wrong date. Also, if you're used to seeing a week or month at a time, you may find it hard at first to use the one- or two-page-per-day formats (and vice versa). If you make a major change in calendars, cut yourself slack as you learn.

Type of fastener is important too. If your planner will travel with you often, get a tab, snap, or zipper closure. Pages get bent and things fall out of open binders.

Another important choice is size. The smaller planners travel well but have little space to write. The larger ones are great on writing space but aren't as portable. Be realistic about what size will best keep you organized and in action.

If you can't tell from online pictures exactly what page layouts look like, visit a retail store or request a catalog to get a better sense before you buy.

Note: Don't take anyone who will be a distraction to the store with you when you shop for a planner. No partners, children, parents, or friends. You're making an important decision. Don't be rushed or intimidated into buying the wrong system for you.

Also keep in mind that retail stores don't carry a full line of any company's planners (except maybe FranklinCovey). If you're not too picky, you can probably find what you want at a retail store. Otherwise, order online.

Turn to the next two pages for a handy guide to the most popular paper planners.

PAPER PLANNERS/ORGANIZERS

	Formats	Where to Find
At-a-Glance **Also Mead, Cambridge, & Five Star**	Daily, weekly, monthly calendars Various sizes Loose leaf & wire bound Open, zipper & tab binders in vinyl & leather Refills & accessories No software The company recommends buying at office supply or stationery stores. They don't carry all products online.	*www.ataglance.com* Available at: Office Depot, OfficeMax, Office City, Office Plus, Staples, Wal-Mart, CVS, Rite Aid, Walgreen's, BJs Wholesale Club, Costco Wholesale, Sam's Club, Kmart, Target, Toys R Us, Best Buy, Barnes & Noble, Borders, Albertson's, Fred Meyer, Meijer, Michaels, Quill, Reliable, Viking
Day Runner	Daily, weekly, monthly calendars Loose leaf 5 sizes 6 styles Open, zipper & tab binders in vinyl, ballistic & leather Refills & accessories No software	*www.dayrunner.com* Also available at: Office Depot, OfficeMax, Staples, Wal-Mart, Barnes & Noble, Meijer, Rite Aid, Grand & Toy, Army & Air Force Exchange Service
Day Timer	1 pg per day 2 pgs per day 2 pgs per week Loose leaf & wire bound 4 sizes Numerous styles Open, zipper & tab binders in vinyl, microfiber & leather Refills & accessories No software Call 800-225-5005 for a catalog	*www.daytimer.com* Also available at: Office Depot, OfficeMax, Staples, Best Buy, Egghead Software, CompUSA, Micro Center, Computer City See also Day-Timers of Canada, UK, & Australia/New Zealand

PAPER PLANNERS/ORGANIZERS (CONT'D)

	Formats	Where to Find
Filofax	2 pgs per week Loose leaf 5 sizes Numerous styles Open, zipper & snap binders in vinyl & leather Refills & accessories Address book software (downloadable, MS Outlook compatible, no returns). Needs special laser paper (3 sizes) Request a catalog online	*www.filofax.com* Also available at: Specialty stationery and higher-end department stores, The Container Store, Mori Luggage. Check web site for stores nearest you. Filofax is also sold in the UK, Canada, Finland, Denmark, Sweden, France, Germany, & Italy.
Franklin Covey	2 pgs per day Loose leaf 4 sizes Numerous styles Open, zipper & snap binders in vinyl, canvas & leather Refills & accessories Desktop and handheld software Online catalog available or call 800-819-1812 Also sells cases & totes	*www.franklincovey.com* Also available at: FranklinCovey retail stores. Check web site for stores nearest you. Sells personal productivity books (mostly Covey) Offers 1-day to 1-wk productivity training (Register online or in-store)
Planner Pad	2 pgs per week Dated & undated Loose leaf & wire bound 3 sizes Open & zipper covers in leather Refills & start date by quarter Accessories (mostly loose leaf) No software	*www.plannerpads.com* Only available online Monthly index tabs are too flimsy if you don't buy a cover

Note: Typical lists are vertical. The Planner Pad works horizontally, funneling weekly lists of activities by categories you choose into daily To-Do lists and appointments.

ELECTRONIC PLANNERS/PDAS

Most people love their PDAs (personal digital assistants). PDAs offer similar features as paper planners — calendar, task list, and notes plus digital extras like photo and document display, games, Web accessibility, and even phone service. Since PDA technology changes rapidly, we don't review specific models here.

Below are PDA pluses and minuses.

Plus	Minus
Many PDAs are pocket-sized and fairly light. Newer models also have cell phone capability, which means you only have to carry one device.	PDAs run on batteries. If your PDA loses its charge, you lose all your data and have to resync it with your computer.
PDA data is easy to update and replace. If you lose your PDA, you have a backup of your data on your computer.	PDAs truncate contact information.

If you allow the PDA to override your computer when you sync, you could lose important data. |
PDAs can store a lot of data (for example, large documents and specialized reference manuals).	Many PDA screens are hard to read, especially for people with less than optimal vision. People with impaired hand coordination may have trouble using the thin PDA stylus.
PDAs work well with schedules that need to be coordinated with others electronically.	
PDAs have alarms to remind you of important activities.	PDA screens can't display a whole calendar week.

PDAs come in a wide range of styles and prices. Unless you're a gadget freak, only buy what you need for your specific purposes. Get a very good PDA if it will be your only planning tool. Get a less expensive one if you only need to carry your contact information.

USE YOUR PLANNER EFFECTIVELY

- Get in the habit of entering things in the appropriate place in your planner, not on stickies or stray pieces of paper.

- Process daily to keep on top of everything and get more done.

- Always carry your planner with you. If you can't do that, carry at least that day's calendar and task list.

- Only carry with you the papers your need for the current day. Gather everything you need the night before.

- Keep your values, vision, goals, projects, and important lists in your planner and refer to them often.

- Keep your planner in good working order (i.e., regularly synchronize and recharge your PDA or refill your paper planner).

- If you decide to use both a paper planner and PDA, don't go overboard. Choose tools that integrate well. Use them as long as they work for you. When they become ineffective, try something else.

NUMBER

6

Set Goals

Goals are results you want to achieve.

YOUR PERSONAL GOALS GIVE DIRECTION to your values and vision. When you align your values, vision, goals, and actions, you accomplish more important things more often.

Writing down your goals is key. Only 3% of adult Americans have specific, written goals. The rest of us wing it. Sometimes, even with vague goals, things work out for us. Often, however, we end up with far less than we'd hoped for or expected.

There's nothing difficult about identifying your goals. The reason most people don't actually commit them to paper and tell others about them is that then they'd be accountable for achieving them. If you're vague about your goals, you don't have to suffer any loss of face if you don't reach them.

Goals can be tangible or intangible. They can be easy or hard, simple or complex, short-term or long-term. Some examples:

- Run a 10K

- Walk 30 minutes a day 5 days a week

- Pay off my debts

- Explore my family tree

- Become a good partner (business, personal)

- Spend more time (with my family, friends, by myself)

- Take three trips a year

- Weigh 140 pounds

- Buy a personal computer

- Buy a company computer system

- Write a book

- Start a business

- Increase my client base by 20%

- Plan my retirement

- Cultivate good employees

- Maximize sales force strength

- Learn how to . . . rock climb, speak Spanish, dance, sing, write, invest, ask for a raise, delegate more, control my anger, give effective feedback, be more assertive, influence others, etc.

The following exercise will help you identify your goals. The next chapter will show you how to turn your goals into a plan for action.

Step 1

The sky's the limit. What would you like to accomplish or have this year? In 5 years? 10 years? 20 years? Your timeframes will depend on your current age.

1. Put **Goals I'd like to pursue** at the top of a piece of paper (or use the space on the next page).

2. Think about all areas of your life (career, home, money, relationships, health, spirituality, personal development, leisure, community, etc.). Go back and look at your values. Then for three minutes write possible goals as quickly as possible. No editing. You aren't committing to what you write, just speculating.

3. After three minutes, look at what you've written. Is anything missing? Does your list suggest any trends that imply deeper goals? If so, add them to the list.

4. Take another few minutes to make any changes.

STEP 2

Take what you've written in Step 1 and edit again, keeping these points in mind.

- Each of your goals needs to state what you'll actually achieve by when. Make them SMART, which stands for:

  - **S**pecific — State your ultimate goal. For example, "Have more energy," or "Look better in my clothes" are more fundamental than "Lose 10 pounds." The weight loss then becomes an action step or interim goal.

  - **M**easurable — Spell out specifically how you'll know you're making progress and how things will look when you've reached your goal.

  - **A**chievable — Realistic for you, given your current situation.

  - **R**ealistic — Stretch, but not so high it's impossible. Otherwise you'll get frustrated and discouraged and give up.

  - **T**ime-Bound — Set a deadline and live it. This gives you a clear target to work towards.

  Example of SMART goals:
  Big Goal – Close $1MM in business this fiscal year
  Supporting Goals – Close 5 deals by 6/1
                  – Finish marketing packet by 2/1
                  – Get feedback on marketing materials by 1/10

- Make your goals results you want to have, not things you want to get rid of (e.g., weigh 180 lbs. vs. lose 30 lbs., become more assertive vs. be less timid).

- Be concise. Make each goal one goal, not a combination of goals.

- Start with the goals that are *most* important to you.

- Postpone or eliminate goals you don't currently have the time or motivation to pursue.

- Have at least one easy and one challenging goal.

- Break big goals into smaller goals so you can create separate goal plans.

- When you finish your goals, list them in your personal planner where you can review them often.

- As you achieve your goals, cross them off and add new ones.

Your values and vision remain only pipe dreams until you translate them into action. Make that focused action, through well thought-out goals, and you've got a 75% guarantee of living your dreams.

We say a 75% guarantee because there are two other important planning pieces you need — an action plan and ways to prioritize your activities so you know what to do when. We cover those in the next two chapters.

NOTES:

NUMBER

7

Plan
Backward

MOST OF US PLAN FORWARD, starting in the present and thinking about what we need to do to reach a goal in the future. Often we don't write anything down. Or we may sketch out just the high points. That's because we'd rather be in action. Planning doesn't seem helpful.

People in project management typically do a much better job of planning. But again, it's usually in a forward direction. And many of them don't use their planning skills outside work.

Planning forward works well for simple, short-term projects (e.g., buying a new TV or booking a vacation). However, it's not as effective if you want to reach complex goals (e.g., finding a new job, losing weight, planning a wedding, or remodeling a house).

The problem with planning forward is that it focuses on actions. Your view into the future is peppered with things you need to do to reach your final goal. But you've got no structured way to figure out how to do them in the right order at the right time.

On the other hand, planning backward focuses on results. It provides the structure you need to get thing done in the right order at the right time. Moreover, it helps you keep up momentum, even when you're not in the mood.

How to Plan Backward

1. Pick one goal. If it's big, divide it into smaller goals. Pick the first one you need to achieve.

2. List the mini goals or milestones you need to accomplish to achieve your goal by the deadline you've set.

3. Draw a time line from left to right. Put the current date on the far left and your deadline on the far right. Insert each milestone with a date, starting from your deadline and working backward.

4. Once your milestones are in the right places, list underneath each one the actions you'll need to take to achieve them. Then keep your plan handy and do what you planned.

Remember, your plan is a dynamic tool to transform your busyness into focused productivity. Take it seriously. Your success and satisfaction depend on it.

NOTES:

NUMBER

8

Prioritize

PRIORITIES AND GOALS ARE CONNECTED. Your goals are the results you want. Your priorities are the important things you do to reach your goals.

Notice we didn't say the important things *you like to do* to reach your goals.

- If your goal is good health and you make it a priority, you might not like getting up at 5 am to go to the gym before work or cutting out dessert each night.

- If your goal is great family relationships and you make it a priority, you might not like missing an outing with your friends so you can attend your aunt's birthday party.

- If your goal is a strong partnership and you make it a priority, you might not like looking at what you do that threatens it.

Without clear priorities, it's hard to reach your goals. Poorly aimed actions rarely hit the bull's eye.

Below are popular ways to prioritize. If you know your values and vision, have set SMART goals, and crafted a realistic action plan, prioritizing should be easy for you.

DO THE MOST IMPORTANT THINGS FIRST

We live in a world of the urgent. If something demands our attention, it usually gets it, no matter what we're already doing.

Occasional urgency isn't a problem. A steady diet of it is. If you feel you rarely have time to do what you really want to do, urgency may be running your life.

Paradoxically, the most important things in life usually aren't urgent. Things like spending time with your family, getting organized at work and at home, exercising, eating well, getting a checkup for yourself or your car, and writing a will or setting up a retirement plan.

Alec Mackenzie (*The Time Trap*) was the first to point out the difference between importance and urgency. Stephen Covey (*First Things First*) expanded the idea in *The 7 Habits of Highly Successful People*.

Covey says we've become addicted to urgency. When urgency takes over our lives, there's no room for importance. He believes typical time management tools and techniques feed our urgency addiction by helping us organize the things we shouldn't be spending much time on in the first place. He depicts these relationships in the matrix below.

COVEY'S TIME MANAGEMENT MATRIX

	Urgent	Not Urgent
Important	**I** • Crises • Pressing problems • Deadline-driven projects, meetings, preparations	**II** • Preparation • Prevention • Values clarification • Planning • Relationship building • True re-creation • Empowerment
Not Important	**III** • Interruptions, some phone calls • Some mail, some reports • Some meetings • Many proximate, pressing matters • Many popular activities	**IV** • Trivia, busywork • Some phone calls • "Escape" activities • Irrelevant mail • Excessive TV [and we'd add computer use]

While we'll always need to be doing things in Quadrants I, III, and IV, Quadrant II is where we should be spending most of our time.

When Covey asked thousands of people what one activity would have significant positive results in their personal and work life, their answers fell into seven key areas:

1. Improving communication with others

2. Better preparation

3. Better planning and organizing

4. Better self care

5. Seizing new opportunities

6. Personal development

7. Empowerment

These are all Quadrant II activities.

MAKE LISTS

All time management experts recommend making lists.

- At a minimum, you need a weekly To-Do list (with no more than 3 or 4 major tasks).

- Many people also have a daily To-Do list.

- In addition, you may want to keep a master list of everything you have to do. You can also add everything you ever want to do. Or you can keep a separate someday/wish list.

- Checklists are also very helpful for frequently recurring activities such as traveling, reports, and shopping.

Use whatever lists work for you but don't let list-making run your life. Our human brains are capable of producing a prolific amount of ideas, all of which we think are gems just because we thought them. But they aren't! Get good at thinking strategically. Cut out the excess and only write down your main priorities. Don't include routine tasks you do automatically.

Note: Small stickies are good for reminders or to schedule tentative appointments in your calendar. However, be careful about relying on them for your whole prioritizing system. They're too easily moved or lost, especially if you carry them around with you.

USE THE ABC SYSTEM

It's a good idea to prioritize your To-Do lists. Many time management folks like the ABC system. Rank each item on your list as either A=high priority, B=medium priority, or C=low priority. To see them easier, group them by letter. *Instead of* using letters, color code your rankings.

Regardless of how you indicate rank, make sure you accomplish your As each day and fill in with the Bs and Cs as you can.

Again, the goal is not to cross off the most tasks on your list. It's to cross off the ones that really matter.

FOLLOW THE 80/20 RULE

Another way to look at priorities is the 80/20 Rule, also known as Pareto's Principle.

In 1906 Italian economist/sociologist Vilfredo Pareto found that 80% of wealth in Switzerland, where he lived, was held by 20% of the people. In the late 1940s American management pioneer Dr. Joseph Juran adapted this economic principle to what he called the "vital few and trivial many."

Common 80/20 examples:

- People wear 20% of their wardrobes 80% of the time

- People read 20% of the newspaper 80% of the time

- 20% of employees take 80% of sick leave

- 20% of customers provide 80% of revenue

- 20% of effort produces 80% of results

We see again that managing your time well and being productive comes from focusing on your "vital few" priorities. In almost anything you do in life, if you can figure out the 20% effort that will lead to 80% of your results, you're definitely headed in the right direction.

OTHER PRIORITIZATION TIPS

- Record your priorities and plans in your organizer so you always have them with you.

- Don't plan too tightly. Identify the fixed points in your day (e.g., appointments, meetings, meals, etc.) and fill in with everything else. Delegate and simplify wherever you can.

- Schedule unpleasant tasks early in the day. You'll feel great to get them out of the way and be free the rest of day to do the things you like. (Mark Twain called this eating your ugliest frog.)

- Defend your calendar. Schedule the important things and then stick to your schedule. Be sure to block out time for your own recreation, play, and personal activities; keep these appointments as sacrosanct as your other appointments. Tell people who ask for your personal time that you're busy. You don't need to explain why.

- Use your peak times wisely. Everyone has a time of day when they have the most energy and think the best. Prioritize your activities so you're doing your most important work then. Do the easier activities when your energy is low.

- Schedule a daily quiet hour. This is another way to use your peak times wisely, minimize interruptions, and take time to reflect. At work, if it's feasible, get your whole office to agree to observe the same quiet hour each day. (If you're the boss, don't try mandating a quiet hour; it never works.)

ASK KEY QUESTIONS

No matter how good you are at setting priorities, sometimes you have to prioritize on the fly.

Get in the habit of regularly asking yourself one or more of the following questions from some of the best time management experts. You'll greatly improve how you spend your time.

- Is what I'm doing this minute moving me measurably closer to my goals?
  —KENNEDY, NO B.S. TIME MANAGEMENT FOR ENTREPRENEURS

- What is the best use of my time right now?
  —LAKEIN, HOW TO GET CONTROL OF YOUR TIME AND YOUR LIFE

- What is the value added from this task?
  —KUNICH & LESTER, SURVIVAL KIT FOR LEADERS

- Is there an easier way to do this?
  —GRIESSMAN, TIME TACTICS OF VERY SUCCESSFUL PEOPLE

- What three to five things can I accomplish today that will make a big difference to the bottom line?
  —RINKE, DON'T OIL THE SQUEAKY WHEEL

ORGANIZE

DISORGANIZATION IS ONE OF THE TOP REASONS people give for poor time management. Living and working amidst clutter can be exasperating — not only for you but also for the people who live and work with you.

This section covers ways to:

- Have a Place for Everything

- Keep a Clean Desk

The benefits of implementing these suggestions are:

- Less upkeep

- Less stress

- Higher productivity

- More time to do what you like to do

- A better outlook on life

Priceless benefits. Go for it!

NOTES:

9

Have A Place
For Everything

ISABELLA MARY BEETON FIRST SAID "a place for everything and everything in its place" in her *Book of Household Management,* published in England in 1861. Both the quote and book have been popular ever since.

In this chapter, you'll find helpful information on how to get organized. Use it according to your needs:

- If you're already fairly well organized, see what else you might do to streamline your process.

- If you're organized in some areas but not in others, focus on what will fill in the gaps.

- If you feel disorganized beyond hope, start here, and/or consult the organizing books we've listed, and/or hire an expert to help you get out from under your mess.

Note: Look for a professional organizer in your local business telephone directory under Organizing Services. Or online at the National Association of Professional Organizers (NAPO) — (847) 375-4746, ***www.Napo.net.*** Most members are American and Canadian, although some live in other countries. You can also search online for professional organizers by country or region.

MANAGE CLUTTER

Owning things has hidden costs. Whether you realize it or not, you pay a mental and physical price to maintain your possessions.

Here are pointers for decluttering:

1. **Schedule regular time to declutter until it's done.** One hour a day or week. Several weekends in a row. Even a week or two of vacation time. Follow whatever schedule keeps you motivated and moving to sort through, throw out, and organize your stuff.

2. **Prioritize your projects.** Declutter one room at a time. If an item in the room you're working on belongs in another room, put it where it belongs but don't start cleaning the second room. Stick with each room until it's done.

3. **Pull everything out first.** Put everything in the room in one place. That will allow you to see how you could better place furniture to accommodate your needs for that room.

   *Exception — if you have a lot of files. Organizing many files takes extra planning and work. See Manage Paper next.

4. **Set up three areas or boxes labeled: Toss, Keep, and Give Away/Sell.** Sort your stuff. As you consider each item, ask yourself the following questions.

- Do I still love it? Does it enhance my life?

- Is it in style?

- Have I used it in the past year?

- Is it reparable/worth repairing?

- Would it be hard to replace?

- Does it have tax or legal implications?

- Do I really need it (not just want it)?

- Would anything bad happen if I didn't have it anymore?

If you can answer "no" to all these questions, get rid of it.

5. ***Get a friend to help you.*** It's a good idea to have someone who's good at organization and isn't a pack rat to supervise your decluttering and provide moral support.

6. ***Learn to let go.*** Hanging on to too much stuff happens for lots of reasons. Things stay in your life because you like them, feel obligated to keep them, or think you might need them in the future. Learn to live with less.

Whatever you own should bring you joy. Notice what increases your energy and what drains it. If you're keeping stuff that reminds you of unhappy or unfortunate times, get rid of it. Someone else may be able to use it without the baggage.

MANAGE PAPER

Unorganized paper is one of the biggest traps to working productively and using time wisely. Like the other things in your life, paper that shows up at your office or house needs a proper place, even if it's in the wastebasket, recycle bin, or shredder.

You've probably heard the old maxim "*Handle each piece of paper only once.*" That's almost impossible to do. But you can handle paper less by following the suggestions below.

When paper shows up, you've got five choices to handle it. Piles aren't one of them. We digress briefly to explain.

No one who works using piles is working productively, no matter what they say. It's impossible to remember where everything is in piles. Even if you know where most things are, you waste time and energy shuffling and reshuffling to find things. In addition, without you no one else can find things quickly. (This includes your assistant; it's a poor use of his or her time to have to search through your piles.) Finally, piles can be a navigation hazard. If you've ever tripped over or slipped on a pile of papers, you know what we mean.

Most time management experts have their favorite acronym for how to handle paper. They're all variations of these five choices:

Toss	Throw it in a wastebasket, recycle bin, or shredder
Delegate	Give it to someone else to do
Do	Act on it (then toss it or file it)
Follow up	Give it a *temporary* home until you need to act on it
File	Give it a *permanent* home where you can find it easily

When you make this approach to paper a habit, you'll automatically whiz through the paper in your life.

More on each below:

Toss

Questions to ask yourself as you consider each piece of paper:

* Do I really need it?

* Will it help me make money?

* Will it be useful when I need it again?

* Is it new information?

* Is it a necessary part of a project or client file?

* Would it be hard to replace?

* Does it have tax or legal implications?

* Would anything bad happen if I tossed it?

If you can answer "no" to all these questions, toss it out.
Other things to toss out:

* Outdated manuals

* Extra/old catalogs, annual reports, and brochures

* Back issues of anything you haven't touched in two years
  (You can usually find it again online if you need it)

* Supporting information for finished projects, including drafts

When you fill out warranty forms (paper or digital), give only contact and product information. Don't answer any marketing questions; you'll stay off marketers' lists and lessen the junk mail you get.

DELEGATE

Perhaps the most powerful action you can take with your paper is giving it to someone else to do. We'll say more about delegation later in Technique #18. For now, consider that just because paper first shows up on your desk doesn't mean you're the most appropriate, or only, person to take action on it.

Do

This is easy.

- If it can be completed in 3 or fewer minutes, do it now.

- If it's truly urgent, do it now no matter how long it takes.

- Otherwise reschedule it for follow up.

FOLLOW UP

The secret to managing papers that require further action is to **schedule them**. That means putting them where they'll show up again when you need them.

Most time management experts recommend using a tickler file. We explain how to set up one on the next page.

Your desktop is NOT a tickler file. When you leave important papers in your in-box or elsewhere on your desk, they're a constant reminder of things you have to do. You're likely to worry that you might forget about them, especially when other important items bury them. Worst case, you **do** forget about them until it **is** too late.

The same goes for bulletin boards. Hanging important papers on a bulletin board is a constant reminder. They can also get lost if you hang up too much. Then they drop completely off your radar screen until it's too late.

Scanning papers and having only a digital tickler file isn't a good solution either. Scanning is time consuming and doesn't work when you need to use original documents and other more "lumpy" things.

Set Up a Tickler File

(Read all instructions before starting)

- Label twelve ⅓-cut file folders January through December.

- Label thirty-one ⅕-cut file folders 1 through 31 (for the most days in any month).

- *Instead* of *the 1–31 folders*, buy a 31–slot tray for the top of your desk or credenza. These come in various materials from inexpensive boxboard to finished wood.

- *Instead* of *the 1–31 folders*, if you work with short follow-up time frames, set up five Monday through Friday folders or five folders for each week in a month (some weeks are split between one month and the next).

- Put the monthly folders in a hanging file in a nearby file drawer, file box, or desktop file rack. Behind the current month put either the daily or weekly folders. Start with the current day forward. For the daily folders, put the days that have already passed behind the next month's folder.

- Keep rotating the weekly folders until you reach the end of the month. As one month ends, put that folder behind the rest of the year's folders and move the next month's folder forward.

- As papers that need follow up cross your desk, put them in the appropriate monthly folder. The first of every month, take out that monthly folder and refile the items in the appropriate daily or weekly folders.

- Each night before you leave your desk, take out the next day's folder and put it on top. The next day, handle all the items in the folder and put the empty folder back in the appropriate place in your tickler file.

  Note: A tickler file is only good if you use it. Until it becomes a habit, put a note in your planner the first of each month to check your monthly folder and a note each day or week to check the daily/weekly folder.

Once you're a regular tickler file user, you'll wonder how you ever survived without one!

P.S. Some time management experts recommend having a C-drawer. Put in that drawer all your lowest priority items (e.g., catalogs, sales brochures, info on things you think you might do someday). Schedule regular times when you tackle some of them. Do, toss, delegate, follow up, or file for future use. Don't leave anything in your C-drawer indefinitely. Then it just becomes clutter.

FILE

Two sobering statistics from time management folks:

1. Most of us use only 20% of the papers we file. (The 80/20 Rule again!)

2. Most of us spend at least 75 hours a year looking for lost papers. That's about 90 minutes a week or 13 minutes a day — a huge amount of wasted time.

Filing overwhelms most people because they don't have a good filing system. Described below are several suggestions for filing, both paper and digital. Use one or a combination, whatever works best for you.

Regardless of system, start with your current papers and email, not your backlog. Otherwise you'll stay behind for a long time.

There are 3 types of files — **Action**, **Reference**, and **Reading**. Action files are the projects you're currently working on. Reference files are those you need to (or want to) keep for future use. Reading files are the articles, etc. you want to read. Everything you keep should fit into one of these three categories, based on frequency of use.

General points:

- Your files should be an information-retrieval resource, not a warehouse. You want a dynamic system that efficiently and effectively serves you.

- It's better to have a few large folders of similar items than many small 1–2-page folders.

- Use file names that make sense to you. For example, Money instead of Finance, Fun instead of Entertainment.

- Keep your most often used files closest to you, within reach without having to get up.

- Create files for future accomplishments (e.g., a trip, your child's education, retirement, buying new technology, a new project on the horizon). Then as information starts to show up, it will already have a home.

- Keep Warranty and Instruction files. If you have many items, group them by category in separate folders.

- Store catalogs in magazine holders. When a new catalog arrives, take a few seconds to pull out the old one and toss it. This easily solves even the worst catalog pile problem. For catalogs you no longer want, call the company and ask to be removed from their mailing list.

- Permanently store important financial records in filing cabinets or banker's boxes, well marked and away from dampness.

- You need to save paper originals even if you also scan.

A chart of financial records to keep is on the next page.

FINANCIAL RECORDS TO KEEP

Category	Record/How Long
Bank Records	• Deposit slips and monthly statements (store with yearly tax documents). • Canceled checks 7 years (fewer is fine in most cases, but why chance it).
Bills	• Shred when payment clears (canceled check comes back or EFT clears). • Big ticket bills for insurance proof permanently.
Birth, Marriage, & Death Certificates	• Permanently
Contracts	• All current contracts. Ask your lawyer about expired contracts.
Credit Card Receipts	• Shred after you get your monthly statement. Keep monthly statements for 7 years. Exceptions: • Keep credit receipts for expense reimbursement or tax deductions permanently. • Keep credit receipts for big-ticket items permanently (to back up warranties).
Health Records	• Current health insurance policy and proof of out-of-pocket expenses (for 2 years).
Home Expenses	• House sale and purchase records, big-ticket item information, and home improvement expenses permanently.
Insurance Policies	• Both current and previous policies (for unresolved claims).
Investments	• Year-end statements permanently. • IRA contribution records permanently. • Annual summaries of 401(K) or other plans until you retire or close the account. • Stock trade confirmations for 7 years.
Military Papers	• Permanently
Pay Stubs	• Reconcile with annual W-2 form. If information matches, shred. If not, demand a corrected W-2c form.
Tax Info	• Backup documentation for 7 years. Keep a copy of your tax return permanently. If you do your own taxes, keep a second copy at another site.
Wills & Trusts	• Permanently

Manage Email

You have the same five choices for managing email:

Toss	Delete it
Delegate	Forward it or give a hard copy to someone else to do
Do	Act on it (then file it or delete it)
Follow up	Give it a *temporary* electronic or paper folder home
File	Give it a *permanent* electronic or paper folder home

Toss

Questions to ask yourself as you consider each email message:

- Will it help me make money?

- Will it be useful if I need it again?

- Is it new information?

- Is it a necessary part of a project or client file?

- Would it be hard to replace?

- Does it have tax or legal implications?

- Would anything bad happen if I tossed it?

If you can answer "no" to all these questions, toss it.

Delegate

Consider that just because a message shows up in your email in-box doesn't mean you're the most appropriate, or only, person to take action on it.

Do

Same choices here.

- If it can be completed in 3 or fewer minutes, do it now.

- If it's truly urgent, do it now no matter how long it takes.

- Otherwise reschedule it for follow up.

FOLLOW UP

Most people leave old messages that need action in their email in-box as new ones pile up. Handle your email in-box like your desk in-box.

CHOOSE ONE of these ways to follow up email:

1. Remind yourself electronically (i.e., drop the email into the Task folder in Outlook or forward it to yourself for receipt later).

    Note: If you get hundreds of legitimate emails a day, check out David Allen's Getting Things Done Outlook Add-In at ***www.DavidCo.com.*** Allen is the author of *Getting Things Done,* which we review on page 118.

2. Put the email into an electronic tickler file. Set up a main folder called Follow Up and 1 through 31 subfolders. (You'll need to put a zero before the single digit numbers — 01, 02, etc.) Then make a habit of checking your electronic tickler file every day, just like your paper tickler file.

3. Print the email (and/or its attachment) and put it in a monthly, weekly, or 1–31 paper tickler file.

FILE

General points:

*   Set up an electronic file system. Duplicate some or all of your paper file names.

*   It's better to have a few large folders of similar items than many small 1–2-email message folders.

*   Create files for future accomplishments. Then as information starts to show up, it will already have a home.

*   Clean out your email folders a few times a year.

NOTES:

NUMBER

10

Keep A
Clean Desk

MOST TIME MANAGEMENT EXPERTS THINK IT'S IMPORTANT to keep a clean desk (as in clutter-free). Some think only uptight people have clean desks. Here's a reasonable rationale for a clean desk. You decide if it makes sense to you.

Your desk is a reflection of your mind. If you're mind is scattered and unorganized, it's bound to show up in the way you keep your physical surroundings. A few time management folks believe every piece of paper on your desk is a decision you haven't made.

When you learn how to work from a clean desk, your productivity increases substantially. You have more space to concentrate and are less anxious and frustrated because you aren't staring at constant reminders of everything you need to do.

Get good at making decisions about your paper quickly.

Points to keep in mind:

- Your in-box is a way station. It's not for long-term storage.

- Use stacking trays for letterhead and your in-box only. Items needing action belong in your action files or tickler file.

- Make room for stacking trays on a nearby shelf or credenza, not on your desk. The same goes for your out-box. Locate it where you (or your assistant) can access it easily.

- Items on your desk may include a stapler, tape dispenser, and Rolodex. Office supplies, including stampers, go inside a nearby drawer or cabinet. A few personal items are okay, but don't overdo it.

- You need a desk at home. Your dining room or kitchen table is NOT a desk. If either (or both) is loaded with mail, projects, and other stuff, do a serious job of decluttering and organizing. If you don't have room for a regular size desk, consider getting a desk armoire that can be closed when you aren't using it.

S E C T I O N   I V

TAKE ACTION

FOCUSING, PLANNING, AND ORGANIZING help you get ready to bring your dreams and ideas into reality. There's nothing more to do but get into action and do the things you've planned to do.

Above all else, good time management is about getting results. When you consistently do what you say you're going to do, magic happens! All kinds of things fall into place to help you succeed.

However, getting things done isn't always easy.

Lots of factors conspire to sidetrack you and waste your time. In this section, we offer advice for dealing with the biggest time wasters.

You'll learn how to:

- Overcome Procrastination

- Learn to Say No

- Be Punctual

- Reduce Information Overload

- Minimize Interruptions

- Do One Thing at a Time

- Take Risks

- Delegate More/Better

- Hold Better Meetings

- Communicate Strategically

We've packed this section with hundreds of helpful suggestions. Start with your biggest problem area(s). Go slow, but be persistent.

11

Overcome Procrastination

CONTRARY TO POPULAR OPINION, procrastination is not a character flaw. Everyone procrastinates at one time or another. Moreover, not all procrastination is bad.

Some things **should** be postponed or put off, temporarily or even permanently. If you're waiting for important information, you're too tired or frazzled to think, or you need to let a new idea incubate, it's okay to procrastinate. Moreover, some seemingly pressing issues have an odd way of completely resolving themselves without any action on your part.

Chronic procrastination, however, can be an annoying, even dangerous habit. Not only does it waste time, it can lead to serious long-term outcomes (e.g., strained relationships, job loss, and poor health).

People procrastinate for many reasons. Time management experts mention the following (in alphabetical order):

- Desire for attention

- Fear of — change, criticism, disappointing others, failure, imperfection, inadequacy, making a mistake, rejection, starting/finishing, success, the unknown

- Feeling overwhelmed

- Indecisiveness

- Lack of a deadline, information, interest

- Overcommitment

- Resentment

- Unclear goals

- Unpleasant or boring task

Procrastination is a symptom of some area of stress for you. It allows you to reduce your anxiety by doing something more pleasurable.

If you want to stop procrastinating, you need to determine why you procrastinate. Then you need to put some new thinking and behaviors into place to combat it. We give some suggestions below.

Note: If procrastination is a big issue for you, you might want to read one or more of the recommended books in our annotated bibliography.

Keep a Procrastination Log

A procrastination log is a special kind of time log that can help you see how postponing things affects you.

1. For one week, focus specifically on what you're doing when you're the most productive and when you're not. When are you late? Feeling overwhelmed? Working too hard and not playing enough?

2. Record both the activities you postpone and the thoughts and feelings that accompany them.

3. Look for patterns. Which of the above reasons for procrastinating seem to apply in your situation?

Tips for Moving Beyond Procrastination

- Break big projects into smaller, manageable chunks. (See Technique #7 — Plan Backward.)

- Start anywhere. Just starting breaks pre-project tension. Finishing will happen if you just keep on starting.

- Use the Swiss Cheese Method — Alan Lakein *(How to Get Control of Your Time and Your Life)* recommends using this method when you have an overwhelming A-project and little time or interest to start it.

  The idea is simple. Get started by poking holes in your project. Do easy, "instant tasks" that take five minutes or less. If one task hits a dead end, try another. A series of instant tasks may not be enough to finish a complex project, but it can help you get a handle on what needs to be done and who will do it.

- Do the hardest, most unpleasant part of the task first. Think of creative ways to get that part done easier and faster.

- Aim for 30 minutes of uninterrupted, quality work a day. Just 30 minutes. Don't force yourself to do more. That will come easily once you're in the habit.

- Set limits. Pace yourself. You will always need time to recharge your batteries, catch up, plan, and reevaluate. Schedule time for those things as well.

- Schedule and stick to one-hour a day recreational/social/play time. Don't sell out on your own needs.

- Remove distractions. If noise bothers you, get a noise-canceling headset.

- Use positive self-talk about your tasks. Saying, "I have to" and "I should" keeps you stuck in a place of blame, helplessness, and depression. Instead, focus on the results you want and say, "I choose to" or "I'm choosing to."

- Aim for excellence. Perfection doesn't exist. Remember the 80/20 Rule. Be pleased with good enough; it's more than adequate for most tasks.

- Celebrate small wins. Give yourself rewards on the way to you big goals. Find a supportive buddy who can celebrate with you and encourage you to stay on track.

If these hints don't help with your procrastination, read one or more of the recommended books in Appendix A and Appendix B. If reading doesn't do it for you and your procrastination has become a big problem for you, seek help from a counselor or therapist.

NOTES:

Learn To Say No

MOST OF US ARE OVERCOMMITTED, by choice or by chance. We've come to equate having a lot to do with feeling important. When there's too much on our plates, our typical solution is to work longer and harder, get less sleep, and give up personal and family time.

But these strategies are a sure set up for future problems — poor health, lost relationships, and a lost sense of purpose.

Overcommitment happens for two main reasons:

- We're unrealistic about how much time projects will take.

- We blindly accept requests from others, especially from those with real or perceived power over us.

The solution to the first issue is better planning. For suggestions on how to allocate your time better, read the chapters in Section II — Plan.

The solution to the second issue is learning to say no.

People who can't turn down requests for their time and energy base their choices and commitments largely on pleasing others. However, being successful is not a popularity contest.

If you did the exercise on time value in Section I — Focus, you know what your time is worth. Don't compromise yourself by frittering away your energy on projects that aren't of the utmost importance to you.

When you allow your time to be abused, you set yourself up for resentment, frustration, and disappointment. When you learn to take a stand for yourself by saying no, these negative feelings disappear.

Here are suggestions for what to say when someone asks you to do something:

1. For someone other than your boss, say either:

   - "I'm sorry, I can't. I've got other priorities right now." If the requester persists, keep giving them the same answer with a smile. They'll eventually get the message.

2. Saying no to your boss is trickier. Bosses assume you can do everything they hand you unless you speak up. Your aim should be twofold: to align your priorities with your boss's priorities and to partner with your boss about your work.

   Here's what to say when your boss asks you to do extra work. Keep in mind that some requests may have to be honored. That's when you need to be flexible:

   - "If I took this on right now I couldn't do it justice because I currently have too much on my plate."

   - "I appreciate your confidence in me but right now I couldn't possibly do it justice with all I have to do."

   - "I'd be happy to do the assignment if you want me working on that rather than on [name the other task(s) you're working on]."

   - "I can do that for you [tomorrow, later this week, next week]."

   - "I can't right now, but perhaps [name] can. He knows more about [the topic]."

3. The most important person you need to learn to say "no" to is YOU.

   – Set goals important to you and then live up to/into them.

   – Don't put too much on your To-Do lists.

   – Decide what you're **not** going to do.

   – If you work at home, treat it like work outside the home. Keep a regular schedule and ask those who live with you to respect it. Dress decently. Arrive and leave every day at the same time. Have lunch away from your desk.

BEING ON TIME IS A BASIC DISCIPLINE of effective time management. People who are punctual create more opportunities for success and goodwill. People who are chronically late miss opportunities and leave a wake of bad feelings behind them that can ripple for days.

Dan Kennedy feels so strongly about punctuality that he devotes an entire chapter to it in *No B.S Time Management*. To him, punctuality is a telling sign of integrity. He says, "People who can't be punctual, can't be trusted" *(p. 40)*. He also believes that if you respect other people's time, they will respect yours.

Kennedy explains that respect of time is linked to respect of opinions, property, rights, agreements, and contracts. Furthermore, respecting time is an indication of people's self-esteem. If they don't trust themselves enough to be on time, why should you trust them?

John Kunich and Richard Lester (*Survival Kit for Leaders*) offer these suggestions for handling the chronically late colleagues in your life:

Coworkers:

- Don't see them when they aren't on time for an appointment.

- Praise them when they are on time.

- Talk to them about their lateness.

- Decrease your association with them if necessary.

Boss:

- Get to know his or her assistant or secretary, who can tell you when the boss is running late.

- Have something to work on while you wait.

Significant other:

- Have something else to do while you wait.

- Tell them an earlier time to be ready, hoping you'll then leave punctually.

- Take separate transportation, if possible.

Note: Different cultures have different approaches to time. If you do business in a foreign country, make sure you know the customs around punctuality and follow them.

14

Reduce Information Overload

MOST OF US ARE SWAMPED WITH INFORMATION. It comes at us from everywhere — TV, radio, the Internet, snail mail, CDs, DVDs, MP3s, at home, at work, on the road. The channels are endless. How can you handle it all?

You can't.

You can only decide what's important and what's not. That's a large part of being able to see both the forest and the trees. What should you focus on? What should you pay less attention to or ignore?

Productivity and time-management expert Jan Jasper (*Take Back Your Time*) says information has no inherent value. Its value comes only when you use it. She offers these steps for decreasing information overload.

1. Recognize that you may be addicted to information. Information may be an addiction for you if:

    •   you have stacks of time-sensitive material you rarely read.

    •   you buy books you forgot you already own.

    •   you get anxious if you can't check the news frequently.

    Hoarding information because you might need it some day is a poor use of your time, energy, and money. You end up feeling guilty and frustrated every time you think about everything you aren't reading, listening to, or using. This includes all the seemingly important files you've got stashed away in file cabinets and computer hard drives.

Realize that much of what passes for news today is sensationalist. The media maw is now a bottomless pit. News may satisfy your voyeuristic tendencies, but it also saps your energy and spreads fear and negativity. Ask yourself if the stress it causes you is ultimately worth it.

2. Change your information-acquiring habits. Take a good, hard look at everything you've saved to read. Toss out the outdated items. Donate or sell old books and magazines. Organize what's left and schedule a weekly reading session.

3. Reduce the flow of new information into your life. Information these days has a brief shelf life.

   – Cancel print and online subscriptions.

   – Get off mailing lists.

   – Take a news break, temporarily or permanently.

   – Tear out articles you want to read and throw away the rest of the newspaper, magazine, or journal. Put the articles in a folder and take it with you to read whenever you have a few extra minutes. Bus, plane, or train. Dentist's office. Standstill traffic jam. Every few months, toss out the unread articles. Read things ASAP if you think they're important. Otherwise, let them go.

   – Learn to skim. Mark as you read with highlighter or pen. When you're done, toss or immediately file the material.

Get into the habit of making conscious choices about the information coming into your life. Whether your unread pile resides on the floor, on a shelf, or in your recycle or trash bin, it's still the same: unread. Filter how, where, and when you get news. Realize that much of it is unimportant and not worth wasting your time and energy on.

Do yourself a big favor and let go of needing so much information. You'll free up physical and mental space for more important things.

NUMBER

15

Minimize
Interruptions

MOST OF US SEE INTERRUPTIONS as big time wasters because they break our momentum and mental focus. The only exception seems to be CEOs, who consider being readily available a large part of their work.

To identify what sidetracks you (assuming you aren't a CEO), write down for one week everything that takes you away from your top priorities. Then figure out what you can do to stay more on task.

Even CEOs might find some of the solutions on the next page helpful:

MINIMIZE INTERRUPTIONS

Interruption	Solution
Email/ Instant Messaging	• Stop checking email compulsively. Only answer it three times a day, early am, before lunch & day's end. • Go offline with IM or turn it off.
Information Requests	• Give people to whom you delegate work sufficient information and authority. • Send a memo to everyone involved. • Honor your promises to get back to people.
Drop-in Visitors	• Say you're busy and set a time to meet later OR state how much time you have and meet. When it's time for the person to leave, say, "That's it, then" or "Thanks for stopping by." • If your desk is located near major office traffic, move it or put up a partition. • Remove a chair by your desk or load it up so there's no room to sit. • Set open-door and closed-door times and make your schedule known. • Meet in someone else's office so you can control your exit. • Be inaccessible. Work from home if you can.
Telephone	• Don't take unscheduled incoming calls. Have set times when you are reachable and when you are not. • Bunch your incoming and outgoing calls. • Give your assistant a VIP list (12 people or fewer). • Call people just before lunch or at quitting time so conversations are short. • Rather than answering, "Hi, How are you?" say "What can I do for you?" or "I can talk for (X) minutes." • Use Caller ID. • Don't have your cell phone on 24/7. Or don't own one.

16

Do One Thing At A Time

MANY OF US THINK THE WAY TO MANAGE our time better and produce more is to multitask. We work on the computer while we talk on the phone. We eat a meal while we work at our desk. We talk on our cell phone while we drive our car and walk on the street.

Laura Stack (*Leave the Office Earlier*) says we've all bought into the **two myths of multitasking**. We think when we work on two or more tasks at once that:

- We're doing more than one thing at a time.

- We're increasing our efficiency and productivity by working more quickly.

In reality, multitasking is moving quickly *between* tasks. None gets our full attention. Research has shown that multitasking actually *reduces* productivity (*Journal of Experimental Psychology: Human Perception and Performance*, vol. 27, No. 4, August 2001). Switching between tasks takes time, even if we aren't aware what our minds are required to do — deciding to switch, switching, engaging with what we switched to, deciding to switch back, and reorienting to what we were doing before we switched.

In some cases multitasking can be dangerous. A recent University of Utah study of people in their early 20s talking on a cell phone while driving showed they had the reaction times of 70-year-olds (*Human Factors*, Winter 2005 issue). And they were using a hands-free phone. What might the statistics be for people using a hand-held phone? Most disturbing, the subjects were considered more impaired than drunk drivers with blood alcohol levels exceeding .08!

A *Wall Street Journal* article on June 15, 2005 on the risk of using cell phones while driving corroborates these findings. The article provides mounting evidence that crashes, near crashes, and evasive incidents are far more likely to be caused by drivers using cell phones.

You'll get more done (and be safer) if you focus on one thing at a time. When you drive, just drive. Pull over to a safe place if you need to talk on the phone. For your work, schedule time in your planner to do important tasks. Then do them one at a time.

If your job naturally entails many brief connections, concentrate fully on each one as it comes up (some call this spotlighting). This is also a very good skill to learn if you have small children. Give whatever you're doing your undivided attention, even if it's for a brief time.

Follow these suggestions for breaking the multitasking habit at work and finishing more in less time:

- Minimize interruptions (see the previous technique).

- Don't obey your every thought. If you remember something you need to do or someone you need to talk to, make a note and do it later, when you've finished the current task.

- Create a communication log for each person you communicate with frequently. When you think of something to tell them, record it on their sheet. When you have several items, call them to set up a time to review the items. Or have a set time each day or week to meet.

- Think results, not activities. Rather than saying to yourself, "I'll work on this report for one hour," say, "By lunch I'll finish two sections of this report." Focus on the outcome you want, not on the process.

- Work standing up occasionally. You'll concentrate more and procrastinate less.

- Give yourself deadlines. If you have too much time, it's easy to become unmotivated and inefficient.

- Plan but don't get paralyzed trying to make everything perfect. Perfect plans don't exist. Success starts with taking your imperfect plans on the road. If something doesn't work out, try something else. No stories. No blame or guilt. Just action and seeing what you get, more action and seeing what you get, etc.

We talk about managing stress in Technique #25. Doing one thing at a time is a good start on cutting down on your stress. Focus and see what happens. You'll be surprised at how much more you actually accomplish.

NOTES:

17

Take Risks

IF YOU WANT TO HAVE MORE TIME and use it better, you need to get out of your comfort zone. Successful people never hide out in safe, secure little ruts.

It's amazing how often most of us sell ourselves out. We easily give in to our unfounded fears rather than go after what we want.

At the end of the day one thing is certain — you'll always get what you're committed to.

If you're committed to feeling comfortable, never looking foolish, and being perfect, you won't accomplish much. Fear will run your life.

If you're committed to your goals, you can do anything. Fear may occasionally pop up, but in spite of it you'll keep moving toward what you want. Do that enough times and eventually fear plays no part in what you do.

Get clear on your commitments. Put a plan in place to fulfill them. And leap!

NOTES:

NUMBER

18

Delegate More/Better

MANY OF US THINK WE'RE THE ONLY ONES who can do a job right. That may be true in some cases. Often, however, there are other "right" ways to do things. Moreover, just because you can do a job better than someone else doesn't make it a good use of your time.

If you have higher priorities that only you can carry out — delegate.

If someone else can do it quicker, better, and cheaper — delegate.

The rewards of delegating far outweigh the risks. You get more time to work on what's important to you. The delegate gets to learn how to be more responsible and effective. Everybody wins.

HOW TO DELEGATE

- Delegation is a kind of teaching. Always explain why and how the task you're delegating should be done. Let delegates know the consequences of a good and bad job. Ask the delegate to explain what's to be done in his or her own words so everyone's clear. Taking the time to be explicit pays off in the long run.

- If you're concerned a person may not be qualified to do the job, give it to someone else, train the person, or replace him or her.

- Make sure your delegates have the tools and resources they need to complete the work effectively.

- Always set a realistic completion date and follow-up milestones. Don't micromanage but do keep tabs on things that are ultimately your responsibility. Keep a folder for each person you delegate tasks to so you'll know what you have in the hopper.

- Expect the best and you'll get it. It's a self-fulfilling process.

- It's okay to pass off small tasks, but don't dump all your mindless activities on others.

- If possible, delegate whole jobs or projects. Others also want opportunities to develop their potential fully and bring more value to their jobs.

- Acknowledge the work your delegate has done, thanking him or her in person, in public if possible. Let your own boss know in a timely manner when one of your delegates has performed well. Write timely thank you notes and letters of appreciation.

- Maintain a business relationship with your staff. It's hard to ask friends to do things they may not want to do. You want to remain objective so you can be fair when it's time to evaluate people's performance.

- If your staff comes to you with problems they want you to solve (upward delegation), give them recommendations and allow them to decide what to do. (This same tactic works well with children!)

Hold Better Meetings

INEFFECTIVE AND/OR UNNECESSARY MEETINGS are big time wasters. Here are helpful tips from time management experts and CEOs:

- Hold only necessary meetings. Cancel ones that aren't. Just because you've scheduled weekly meetings doesn't mean you have to meet every week. Often your business can be better handled another way, like a conference call, memo, or individual meetings.

- Hold meetings in atypical places — at the site of issues being discussed (e.g., production floor, warehouse), at a local low-key restaurant, in a created fun/fantasy setting.

- Schedule meetings at 11 am or 4 pm. People will be more focused and wrap up thing quickly so they can leave for lunch or home respectively.

- Don't serve food. It adds unneeded cost, calories, and distraction.

- Invite only the critical people. Five to eight is an optimum number to reach decisions and get things done. After the meeting, distribute an FYI memo to others who need to know.

- Distribute an agenda at least a day in advance. Be specific about what will be discussed. Broad, unstructured topics usually lead to aimless discussions and feelings of spinning wheels and déjà vu.

- Assign times to each agenda item and stick to them. Put the most important items in the middle-third of the meeting. Before that, people are still getting present. After that, they're running out of steam and thinking about what's next after the meeting.

- Manage agenda-busting. Don't allow unexpected issues that can be handled later to derail your meeting. Assign a person or ad hoc group to look into the matter further and report back.

- Start and stop on time. Don't reward latecomers by starting later or giving them a recap of what they've missed. Remove empty chairs once you start and require latecomers to stand. Or lock the door so latecomers can't come in. Or have latecomers pay a financial penalty. Soon people won't be late.

- Put time limits on how long people talk, but don't restrict the free play of ideas. Have someone besides the meeting convener be a timekeeper.

- Leverage the thinking in the room. Ask strategic questions to draw out better ideas (e.g., What do you think worked best? What are the pitfalls or challenges?). Play Devil's Advocate.

- Make reports executive summaries, 1 page max. Provide supporting data after the meeting for anyone who wants to read it.

- Leave no loose ends. Every topic discussed needs closure, even if it's to table it until the next meeting or discard it.

- Give a 10-minute warning before the meeting ends.

- Shortly after the meeting, send out a brief report of decisions made and who agreed to do what by when. Hit the high points; don't include detailed "he said, she said" descriptions.

- Follow up on outstanding items.

- Use the previous meeting report at the next meeting to track progress on actions.

- Stay alert to what's working and what isn't. Don't be afraid to drop old ways of meeting and try new ones.

NOTES:

20

Communicate Strategically

THE INCREASING NUMBER OF COMMUNICATION CHANNELS these days is a mixed blessing. We have lots of options, which means we also have more responsibility, not less, to communicate well.

Below we cover the most common communication channels — computer, telephone, and fax, with additional comments on the wise use of electronics in general.

EMAIL

We covered organizing email in Technique #9 — Have a Place for Everything. Below are rules for better email communication from Laura Stack (*Leave the Office Earlier*) and Jan Jasper (*Take Back Your Time*).

1. Keep messages brief and focused — No one has time to wade through long, meandering streams of consciousness. Get to the point quickly. Be thorough in your responses. Edit carefully before you send. Don't include too many topics; write several brief emails if necessary.

   The same goes for replies. Say what you need to say concisely. Often "Thanks!" or "Got it" is enough.

Note: It takes longer to type an email than to say the same thing on the telephone. If you want a quick response, call.

2. Keep your message style simple — Use sentence case. It's what everyone's used to reading. All lowercase looks lazy. All uppercase is perceived as shouting. Also follow normal grammar, spelling, and punctuation rules, especially if you're communicating with customers or clients. Asterisks make selected words stand out (*very*). Or bold them, but don't overdo it. Also don't use lots of colors and graphics. Some email programs can't read HTML.

3. Use the Copy option appropriately — Use BCC (blind copy) only when you're sending a message to a large distribution list. This saves recipients from having to scroll through many names. It also saves them from receiving unwanted Reply to All messages. Don't use BCC to hide recipients from the main recipient; it's dishonest. CC anyone else who you want to see the message.

4. Show contents and priority in the Subject header — Use short subject titles. You can also use agreed upon acronyms; e.g., AR for Action Required or MSR for Monthly Status Report.

5. Use a signature — Always include complete contact information at the end of your email, including Web address. Most email programs can do this for you automatically.

6. Summarize forwarded messages — Reading through a long list of forwards is annoying. Include only relevant parts of the original email(s) in your replies. Never edit someone else's words without asking their permission first.

7. Check out virus warnings and chain letters before forwarding them — Don't contribute to useless information clogging up the Internet. Good hoax sites include: ***www.Snopes.com, www.TruthorFiction.com,*** and ***www.Tafkac.org.***

8. Be selective about the emails you receive from friends — If someone is sending you too many jokes and stories, ask to be removed from their list. Tell them it isn't personal; you just have too much email to handle.

9. Communicate face-to-face or by phone for confidential, emotional, or complicated messages — Using email in these instances can often make situations worse. No matter how well worded your email, it can't convey the proper tone of a voice conversation. Emoticons (smileys) are a poor substitution — and they look unprofessional.

10. Remember: your email isn't private — If you work for a company, your email is company property. Be careful about what you send. You could be fired or prosecuted for sending off-color or personal email. In addition, if you're email isn't encrypted, it isn't secure. *Don't write anything in an email that you wouldn't put on a snail mail postcard.*

VOICE MAIL

Voice mail is faster than email and more easily checked when people aren't at their desks. Also, some people don't check their email frequently. Here's advice on how to leave an effective voice mail message from Stack, Jasper, and John Kunich & Richard Lester (*Survival Kit for Leaders*).

1. Plan what you want to say — It cuts down on the time someone has to listen to your message and insures you get heard better.

2. Be brief — Your message should last 30 seconds or less.

3. Leave a specific message — Never say, "Hi, this is [your name]. Give me a call," even if you know the recipient well. Say in detail what you're calling about. For people who don't know you, begin and end with your name, company, and phone number, speaking slowly. Pause as you say your number, e.g., 407 (pause), 553 (pause), 1207.

4. If an assistant answers and the person you're calling is unavailable, ask to leave a voice mail. The person you're calling will get your message directly rather than filtered through a third party and can listen to it more than once.

5. Watch your voice volume, tone, and enunciation — Don't talk too loudly or too softly. Sound energetic. Smile while you leave your message; people can hear it. If you want your call returned, don't sound sarcastic or irritated.

6. Learn your voice mail system — You'll save a lot of time knowing how to speed up and slow down messages, skip to the end, delete, forward, and automatically reply.

7. Avoid telephone tag — Give the people you call and the people who call you suggestions for times when you can be reached. If you make phone appointments, keep them or reschedule.

Telephone Calls

Stack, Jasper, Kunich & Lester, and Stephanie Winston (*Organized for Success*) offer the following advice on productivity on the phone. See Technique #15 — Minimize Interruptions for other suggestions.

1. Prepare a script or outline prior to important or complex calls. This insures you cover all points and stay on topic.

2. Keep focused — When the conversation wanders, gently bring it back to your agenda.

3. Get callers to come quickly to the point — Warmly say, "What can I do for you?" or "How may I help you?"

4. If the answerer is a gatekeeper, explain the nature of your call briefly until you've been transferred to the right person. When you reach that person, get his or her direct phone number so you won't have to go through a gatekeeper again.

5. Return phone calls as quickly as possible, no later than 24 hours, even if it's to say you can't talk until a later time.

6. Prioritize your return calls — Just because you like talking with certain people doesn't mean you should call them first if other calls have higher priority.

7. Call high-ranking people very early in the morning or after normal business hours. You're likely to reach them directly.

8. When you're out of town, schedule a daily conference call with your staff — Save time by covering everything only once.

9. Give out only your landline number. Have it forwarded to your cell phone when you're out of the office and filter with Caller ID.

10. Buy a headset — Protect your neck, shoulders, and back and work hands free. Invest in a wireless headset and you can also move around your office when you're on the phone.

FAX

1. Rising email spam filters make faxes a fast, simple way to send messages these days. Also, people tend to put more thought into what they write in a fax than in an email. If you're more visual than auditory, you may like faxes better than voice mail.

2. Consider faxing someone you can't reach by phone. If you can fax from your computer, all the faster.

ELECTRONICS IN GENERAL

Time management books published before the technology explosion don't have advice on electronics use (unless they've been updated and reissued). Even most new books don't cover the subject well.

Electronics don't always save time and increase productivity. An obsession with electronic devices can lead to many time wasters; namely, procrastination, interruptions, and poor communications.

Use these questions to help you think about your use of electronics. They apply to any kind of electronic gizmo you may own (TV, radio, computer, fax, PDA, cell phone, audio and video players, DVR).

- Do I frequently interrupt or avoid conversations with others to use this device?

- Does using this device ever bother other people?

- Do I spend more time with this device than with the significant others in my life?

- Am I lost without regular access to this device?

If you answered yes to even one question, you may be addicted to electronics. You may not see it as a problem, but if your family, friends, or coworkers do, seriously consider changing how you use your time. To update a familiar quote, "No one on their deathbed ever wished they'd [watched more TV, spent more time on the computer, faxed more, talked on the phone more, listened to more music, watched more recorded programs, or played more video games].

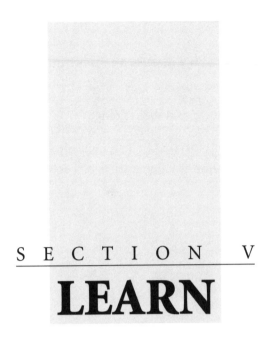

SECTION V

LEARN

WOULDN'T IT BE GREAT IF YOU COULD follow time management advice like a food recipe? Just do what it says and voila! Your life turns out like a perfect chocolate soufflé. That doesn't usually happen, however. People are much less predictable than food ingredients.

Most of us are great pretenders. We say we want to grow personally and professionally, get organized, work fewer hours, eat better, exercise, spend more time with our family, travel, and a host of other things. But we rarely do any of them in a clear, committed way.

As you put in place better time management practices, you need to learn what is working and what isn't. In this section we offer four ways to find that out:

- Experiment

- Review and Reflect

- Measure Results

- Give and Get Feedback

We conclude with a discussion on the importance of taking good care of yourself.

- Manage Stress and Well-Being

Each strategy in this section can help you be your best — if you consciously put them into regular practice until they become life-long habits.

21

Experiment

A UNIQUE WAY TO LEARN about managing time better is to experiment. Most of us think our typical ways of doing things are unchangeable. We say, "That's just the way I am" or "that's just the way things are." We accept the status quo without question.

Experimenting puts you in the driver's seat of your own learning. Nobody else has to know what you're up to.

Here are some experiments to try:

1. Observe yourself. What do you say? What do you do? What responses do you get? No judgment. Just watch yourself to become more aware of how you operate.

2. Practice spotlighting. Be totally present to each task you do (including conversations). Focus intently until you're done. Then focus on the next task. And the next. See where and when your attention wants to wander.

3. Get out of your own head and appreciate things from different perspectives. Ask questions. Ask for advice — without automatically censoring what you hear.

4. Live "off peak" — Don't do things at the same time everyone else does them. Commute outside of rush hour. Shop when the stores aren't crowded (or buy more online). Eat out earlier or later.

5. Do something new on a regular basis — Never had Thai or Vietnamese food? Give it a try. Always seek out a familiar face at a party? Start a conversation with someone you don't know. Always take the same route to shop or go to work? Try another route. Sure, it may be longer, but it will open your eyes to new things along the way.

6. Let past decisions and experiences go. Learn your lessons and move on without beating yourself up or blaming others.

   Note: We know a wise manager who says she never questions her past decisions because she knows that at the time, she made the best decision she could. Sure, if she knew then what she knows now, she might have made a different decision. But that's not how life works. She doesn't waste time worrying.

7. Build self-discipline. Alan Lakein (*How to Get Control of Your Time and Your Life*) suggests this gradual approach:

   – Start with an easy situation. Say you decide to do get up early to walk but then stay in bed instead. Rather than blaming yourself, take credit for your decision. You chose it.

   – Next, find something small about the situation you can change. For example, put your walking shoes by the bed. When your alarm goes off, put them on, take a few steps, take them off, and go back to bed. Your choice.

   – The next day, up the ante. Walk out into the hall. Then go back to bed. You get the idea.

   – No matter what you do, always make yourself right. Soon you'll notice your relationship to both choices changing.

   – Within three to six weeks, you will have developed the internal desire to make good use of your time, even in the face of tasks you don't want to do.

- Once you've built willpower on easier tasks, tackle harder ones. Again, use the gradual approach.

8. Practice trial and success. Lakein also says making mistakes is the only way to succeed. Endlessly weighing pros and cons for fear of doing it wrong is a big waste of time. Instead, jump in. Be willing to accept failures as your dues for eventual success.

   Successful people like Thomas Edison, Albert Einstein, Marie Curie, and Abraham Lincoln all failed for years before they succeeded. Look what we would have missed if they'd given up.

Experiment. Eventually, doing what's most important will easily win out. You won't even have to think about it.

NOTES:

22

Review & Reflect

MANAGING TIME IS A DYNAMIC PROCESS. Your systems won't work effectively for long if you don't keep tabs on them and regroup when necessary. To stay productive, you need regular review and reflection.

Most time management experts recommend a Weekly Review. Many also recommend a Daily Review. Neither has to take much time. At least once a year you should also review your values and vision.

WEEKLY REVIEW

Do your Weekly Review at the same time on the same day, if possible. If you're a manager, best-case scenario is 1–2 hours early Friday afternoon. That way you still have time to act if something turns up that needs immediate attention. Other popular times are Sundays and during plane or train trips if you travel often.

Things to do in your review:

- Corral bits of stashed info (notes, business cards, brochures, receipts, etc.).

- Process your notes and enter them into the appropriate place later reference. Toss what you no longer need.

- Look at recent calendar items for remaining actions. Look at upcoming calendar items for things you need to prepare. Add these actions to your lists.

- Evaluate projects for completed and next actions.

DAILY REVIEW

Do your Daily Review at the end of each day. It should include a quick glance at your calendar, tickler file, and action lists (calls to make, work to do on your computer or around your office or house, errands, etc.). Locate loose ends and prepare for the next day.

VALUES AND VISION

Our lives change, often without our noticing it. Make sure your values and vision match the life you're currently living. If not, realign your life to your old values and vision or rework your values and vision to match your new life. Your values and vision are a fundamental part of you. Don't sell out on yourself, regardless of what others think.

Give &
Get Feedback

A CRUCIAL ELEMENT OF EFFECTIVE TIME MANAGEMENT is communicating with others in ways that coordinate action and allow everyone to perform well and get things done. This is the essence of feedback.

While the word "feedback" can trigger negative associations for some people, feedback isn't inherently negative and can be used in many positive ways.

GIVING FEEDBACK

Giving feedback can be both formal and informal.

The most popular formal feedback is the performance appraisal. Performance appraisals are designed to help people learn what's working, what's not, and how they can change their behavior to be more effective. Performance appraisals are usually done once or twice a year.

However, it's not a good idea to rely solely on formal performance feedback for two reasons:

- Employee ratings are frequently overinflated.

- Once or twice a year doesn't provide employees enough information or opportunity to change.

Adding regular *informal* performance feedback can be very helpful. The following suggestions come from Kunich & Lester (*Survival Kit for Leaders*).

- Timing is important. So is frequency. Give feedback soon after behavior occurs. This allows you to handle fewer issues and improve the chances of positive learning.

- Explain performance standards, areas of responsibility, and expectations to new employees as soon as they start a job.

- Give specific, provable examples when delivering feedback. Providing overwhelming evidence only raises defensiveness. People can feel attacked and unjustly criticized.

- Praise people for a job well done and a positive attitude. Be specific ("The client reported you handled her complaint well") rather than general ("You did a nice job").

- Support people to overcome areas of difficulty.

- Be accurate and clear. Don't hide, sugarcoat, or soft-pedal information an employee needs to hear.

- Be kind. Only give feedback on things over which people have control. This applies both to personal abilities and areas of responsibility.

GETTING FEEDBACK

Most of us like giving feedback when we're asked. When the shoe's on the other foot, however, we'd rather boil in oil. Voluntarily ask somebody else how they think we're doing? "No, thanks. I already know I'm doing fine."

It's hard for many of us to admit that we don't know everything. So we keep pretending that we do and therefore don't need anyone else's input.

Successful people, however, readily admit they don't know everything. They use their lack of knowledge as a source of strength. As a result, they're better at listening to others, owning up to mistakes, getting feedback, and moving on without lingering doubts or hard feelings.

By embracing their ignorance, they paradoxically demonstrate their wisdom and put themselves on the path to getting what they want.

Getting feedback can be both formal and informal too. The formal route is the receiving end of a performance appraisal. As we said, performance appraisals have their place. But one of the best ways to find out about yourself is to actively seek *informal* feedback from others by interviewing them.

INTERVIEWS

1. Set up individual face-to-face interviews with at least three people who know you well. Tell them that you want to learn more about yourself and would like to ask them a few questions to get their honest feedback.

2. If you can't meet face-to-face, talk on the telephone. DO NOT do your interviews via email. It's too impersonal.

3. Find a quiet spot where you won't be interrupted for 10–15 minutes. Explain that you'll ask a question and then just listen. The only time you may talk is if you need clarification on something the other person has said. Otherwise, make no assessments about what they're saying. It's a good idea to take notes as they talk so you'll remember the conversation.

4. Ask each person some or all of these questions:

   - What do you think I'm really good at?

   - What do you think I need to improve?

   - What's most important to me?

   - What talent or ability do I have that I don't use?

   - What's my best-kept secret?

   - What's my biggest complaint?

   - What can you count on me for?

   - What can't you count on me for?

5. When you're done, thank them for sharing their thoughts.

6. After you've had time to think about what they've all said, acknowledge yourself for the strengths they mentioned and figure out how to approach your areas of improvement. Don't rest on your laurels. To

paraphrase an old saw — "If you always do what you've always done, you'll always get what you've always gotten."

Used appropriately and respectfully, feedback is a very useful tool. Learn to get good at both giving and receiving it and many of your time management problems will diminish or disappear.

24

Measure Results

ONE OF THE MOST DIFFICULT ASPECTS of effective time management is holding yourself and others accountable for achieving results. To do that, you need measurable yardsticks.

Your SMART goals are your most important yardsticks. If you've designed your goals correctly and acted on them, measurement is easy. Either you did what you said you'd do by a specific date or not.

Your promises are other measurable yardsticks. Either you keep them or you don't. If you don't make them in the first place, you've got nothing to measure. And lots to lose.

Most of us are uncomfortable with this level of accountability. Not only do we repeatedly let ourselves off the hook for producing results, we allow others to do the same. This "accountability conspiracy," which pervades many organizations, is an unconscious collusion that promotes mediocrity.

If measuring results isn't your strong suit, pick an easy SMART goal and achieve it. Then repeat the process until you're hitting closer and closer to the bull's-eye on your all your targets, including the big ones.

As for promises, try this exercise to reinstate power to places in your life where you've lost it:

- Identify 1–2 places where you're not following your own advice or slipping up.

- Come clean about this to yourself and others, if appropriate.

- Re-promise. Then honor them like your life depended on it. It does.

You can look at life as a game. Every game needs a scorecard. If you aren't measuring something, the game isn't a game. It's just time passing by. Whatever they are, have goals and promises that mean something to you. That's your game. Only you can play it.

25

Manage Stress & Well-Being

WE PUT THIS TECHNIQUE LAST for two reasons:

1. If you followed most of our advice up to now, your life should automatically be less stressful. You should be feeling better mentally, physically, and emotionally.

   (If your life isn't less stressful, you either skipped to this chapter first or only read the book. If it's the former, read on. If the latter, now that you know what to do, go back and do it.)

2. Managing time is a dynamic process. It requires frequent review and reevaluation. The 25 tools and techniques presented in this book are really a circle. This chapter is both the end and the beginning.

Odd as it may be, most time management books don't say much about stress and well-being. Yet worldwide, numerous surveys and studies show workplace stress at an all time high and health care costs skyrocketing.

According to The American Institute of Stress (*www.Stress.org*), stress-related illnesses now cost the US over $300 billion a year. Other countries report comparable figures.

Most work stress is attributable to job insecurity, increased psychological demands, changing demographics, and other economic and political factors. As the boundaries between work and personal life continue to blur, we're paying a high price for being available 24/7.

What does this mean for you? It's a good news/bad news scenario.

The bad news — too much stress will eventually burn out your immune system. Sooner or later an impaired immune system leads to diseases like arthritis, heart disease, diabetes, and cancer. You could have a heart attack or stroke and die young. Or worse, you could live many years with multiple health problems and reduced quality of life. Blunt, but those are the facts.

The good news — stress isn't something that just happens to you, without your participation. You play an active part in how you perceive and experience stress. This means you have a good deal of control over it, even if you can't control much of what goes on around you. It turns out that most of your well-being is in your hands.

Below we offer strategic ways to take charge of the your well-being and stress. Although they're brief, please take them seriously. They work, even if at first they seem simplistic or far-fetched.

REFRAME YOUR PERCEPTION OF TIME

Develop a flexible relationship to time.

Small efforts often count more than big ones. Spotlight small chunks of time. Make 10 minutes important rather than thinking you need more time to get something done. Congratulate yourself for whatever you've accomplished rather than berating yourself for not having gotten to what you haven't done.

TAKE A BREAK

Contrary to conventional wisdom, you can't always think your way out of difficult or pressing situations. Often the answers come faster and easier when you do something else. Stories abound of successful people who attribute much of their success to letting sticky problems simmer while they nap, take walks, or do other mundane things.

Taking a break can be short and informal or longer and more focused. Both are important.

- You probably already take short 5–10 minute breaks during your workday to do things like surf the Internet, play computer games, do a crossword puzzle, read something not related to work, stare out the window, or call someone. Or you might listen to music, stretch, or take a short walk. Whatever you do, make sure it's relieving your stress, not adding to it.

- Longer breaks allow your mind and body to reconnect. We all know that regular aerobic exercise like jogging, bicycling, walking, dancing, and swimming helps reduce stress. But so does spending personal quiet time each day in meditation or prayer or doing yoga, tai chi, or qi gong. All have a valuable calming, integrating effect on the body/mind.

- Whatever you choose to do, do it because it gives you more energy, clearer thinking, and the prospect of a longer, healthier life. No other reason will provide the motivation to keep you at it long-term.

- Take a real vacation. Even if you don't leave home, limit your contact with work or cut it off completely.

- Eat smaller meals more often. It'll keep your blood sugar stable and prevent overeating.

Fly Smart

Air travel is now routinely stressful. Follow these tips from veteran flyers to make your trips more enjoyable.

- Never take the last plane out if you can avoid it. If your flight is cancelled, you're stuck overnight at a hotel or the airport.

- Always carry backup flight information. If your flight is cancelled, call the airline to rebook rather than wait in a long counter line.

- Take only what fits in carry-on luggage. Ship ahead if you need to take more. If you can't ship ahead, pack your most necessary, valuable items in your carry-on. Then if your checked luggage is delayed or lost, you're still functional.

- Being captive miles above the ground in a speeding metal tube is not a natural human environment. Your body knows it. When you fly:

  - Drink 8 oz. of water, preferably bottled, every hour.

  - Don't drink alcohol or caffeine. Both contribute to dehydration. Also, the debilitating effects of alcohol doubles every 10,000 feet.

  - Walk around or stretch your legs every hour to maintain good circulation and avoid blood clots.

  - Minimize exposure to unhealthy recirculated air by not aiming the air vents at your face and wearing a personal negative ion generator.

  - Don't do work from take off to touch down. (This little heresy is ours.) Whatever you might accomplish by working every second of your flight isn't worth the chipping away at your health that it causes. Most people don't see this, or don't want to see it.

FIND BALANCE

Many people talk about finding work/life balance. We don't separate the two. Work/life balance presumes that you can optimize both your work and personal lives. Many people, including time management experts and university researchers, don't believe that's possible.

Here are general observations about balance:

- Balance is about managing your commitments and energy. When you're clear about your values, vision, and goals, you tend to do less. Learn to let go of the 80% "trivial many."

- Balance is different for everyone. Spend time discovering what it means to you and crafting a schedule that honors it. If you live with other people, enroll their help too.

- Slow down and get back in touch with yourself on weekends (or whenever you have days off from work). If you work at home, close up shop and stay away. Resist the temptation to use your computer, fiddle with your files, or read business material.

- Consciously choose to do nothing. Putter, talk a stroll, sit in the park, or play with your pets.

- Get 7–8 hours of sleep a night. Seek help if you have trouble sleeping.

- Make sure you have enough social support. You need at least one or two other people who you trust and can share life's ups and downs with regularly.

✳   ✳   ✳

In the end, time management is really self-management. To be successful you've got to take a stand for what's important to you and actively pursue it, not just dream about it.

"Many people fail in life, not for lack of ability or brains or even courage but simply because they have never organized their energies around a goal."
—ELBERT HUBBARD
WRITER & CRAFTSMAN, 1856–1915

Get a goal, get organized, and get in to action. Your relationship to time, and your stress levels, should improve dramatically.

NOTES:

Appendix A

The Best Time Management Books — Annotated

- Books are listed in ***descending order,*** based on Amazon.com reviews as of June 15, 2006 and our own assessments (we read them all from cover to cover). We researched many more books than appear here. If a book isn't on the list, we didn't think it was worth recommending.

- Books with more Amazon reviews weren't necessarily better. A more telling indicator was the *average reviewer rating* (on a 5-star scale with 5 = highest).

- *Note #1:* We don't personally know any of the authors and didn't strike any deals to give anyone a better review.

- *Note #2:* Duplicate reviews and obvious reviews by the books' authors were excluded from final tallies.

- *Note #3:* Many of these books are also available in CD, cassette, and/or MP3 formats. Audio versions are usually abridged (shortened), so check before you buy. Good audio web sites include ***www.Audible.com, www.AudioQueue.com, and www.SimplyAudioBooks.com.***

1. **How to Get Control of Your Time and Your Life** by Alan Lakein. Signet. Originally published in 1974. Reissued edition February 1989. 160 pgs, paperback (47 reviews, 4.9 stars).

   Upside — Reviewers called this a short, easy read. They said the book was practical, wise, and life changing. Some who had read it years ago said it was still a masterpiece and a great reference. A few gave the author kudos for accommodating the quirks of human nature. Many recommended giving the book as a gift.

   Downside — Some noted that a few examples were dated and the book was written before two-career families came on the scene. They had no criticisms of Lakein's advice.

   Our Take — This book is well-written, easy to carry in a pocket or purse, and offers a proven, simple process for managing your life. The examples are very helpful. Even the dated ones don't take away from Lakein's points. We excluded a 1-star rant that made no sense given the mainly superlative reviews.

2. **Take Back Your Time: How to Regain Control of Work, Information, and Technology** by Jan Jasper. St. Martin's Griffin, November 1999, 243 pgs, paperback (11 reviews, 4.9 stars).

   Upside — Reviewers said the book was well-organized, well-written, and offered practical, helpful solutions. Several liked the author's fresh perspective on being organized.

   Downside — None mentioned.

   Our Take — We agree with the reviewers. The author hits all the important areas of time management in an entertaining, engaging way. Lots of useful "aha" insights. Excellent book for everyone, with information on both the corporate and home office and the family. Some resources are dated but the list is still good.

3. **Leave the Office Earlier: The Productivity Pro Shows You How to Do More in Less Time . . . and Feel Great About It** by Laura Stack. Broadway Books, May 2004, 300 pgs, paperback (11 reviews, 4.9 stars).

Upside — Ten glowing reviews.

Downside — One reviewer said the author has no real world work experience and covered many topics too briefly and simplistically.

Our Take — This is a well-organized book for people who work (at home or not). Using categories representing the first letters of the word "productive," the author presents 10 tight chapters loaded with valuable tips on how to manage personal productivity. The writing is clear and entertaining. You can take a productivity questionnaire repeatedly to track your progress.

4. **No B.S. Time Management for Entrepreneurs: The Ultimate No Holds Barred Kick Butt Take No Prisoners Guide to Time Productivity & Sanity** by Dan Kennedy. Entrepreneur Press, July 2004, 180 pgs, paperback. (17 reviews, 4.7 stars).

   Upside — Most reviewers loved the book. Many gave examples of how following the advice in this book had skyrocketed their productivity and income.

   Downside — One reviewer was disappointed there was no advice on time management for a successful family/personal life. Another thought Kennedy came across as arrogant and judgmental.

   Our Take — Most reviewers said they were already Dan Kennedy fans, an eager bunch that gobbles up everything Kennedy sells. With good reason; Kennedy's ideas work. However, this book isn't for everyone. Kennedy's approach to managing time is ruthless. Take it or leave it. This isn't a comprehensive time management system, but the book is clearly written and engaging with sound advice. People who aren't entrepreneurs will also find it useful.

   *The next two books on leadership each include a chapter on time management. Both books are full of excellent advice to help leaders and their teams be more productive.

5. **Survival Kit for Leaders: An Interactive Way for a Leader to Become and Stay a Survivor** by John Kunich & Richard Lester. Skyward Publishing, March 2003, 222 pgs, paperback (26 reviews, 4.7 stars).

Upside — Many reviewers found this book practical, inspirational, and suitable for leaders in all walks of life. They liked the tight, no-fluff, humorous writing, and comprehensive treatment of leadership. Several thought the time management chapter was outstanding.

Downside — One reviewer thought the book had too many "silly metaphors and clichés." Another thought the reviews were stacked with self-serving recommendations.

Our Take — This is a transformational book. The time management information is brief but focused and covers aspects of time, like watching TV, not mentioned in other books.

6. **Don't Oil the Squeaky Wheel: And 19 Other Contrarian Ways to Improve Your Leadership Effectiveness** by Wolf Rinke. McGraw-Hill, April 2004, 224 pgs, paperback (10 reviews, 5 stars).

    Upside — Reviewers said this was a common sense, easy read. They liked the author's lighthearted treatment and refreshing approach to leadership.

    Downside — None mentioned.

    Our Take — The author is a long-time management consultant numerous published books and articles. This book offers no-nonsense advice on a wide-range of management practices in a frank, humorous way. Examples are compelling. A good management primer, including the chapter on productivity and time.

7. **The Procrastinator's Handbook: Mastering the Art of Doing It Now** by Rita Emmett. Walker & Co., September 2000, 224 pgs, paperback. (52 reviews, 4.5 stars).

    Upside — Reviewers thought this book was written in a light, friendly, readable way and offered quick, practical tips. Most liked the down-to-earth, we're-all-in-this-together tone and the inspiring quotes at the end of each chapter.

    Downside — Some reviewers thought the book was a collection of tips rather than a step-by-step handbook. They said it had too much "why" and not enough hard-hitting fix-it advice. Some didn't like the pep-talk tone. Others thought it presented only clichés. Some thought the book was disorganized.

Our Take — This is a fun, easy read with useful explanations and ideas about procrastination, but the book isn't well organized. If you follow the author's advice as you read, you may do some things first that would be better left until after you've done others presented later. We like the no-pressure extra credit exercises at the end of each chapter. They offer different ways to get in touch with what's important to you and why you procrastinate.

8. **The Time Trap: The Classic Book on Time Management** by Alec Mackenzie. AMACOM. Originally published in 1972. 3rd edition, July 1997, 282 pgs, paperback (17 reviews, 4.5 stars).

Upside — Reviewers respect Mackenzie's 30+-year career as a time management expert. They liked the book's to-the-point, practical advice on how to move beyond the top 20 time wasters.

Downside — One reviewer complained that the book is mainly for managers in large organizations. Another said it didn't offer an overall time management system.

Our Take — The book presents no-nonsense advice on time management at work. Most of the book is short, practical chapters on time wasters. The writing is a bit dry and some ideas are dated but otherwise this is a good manual for managers. If you don't work in a complex organizational environment, you probably won't find enough here to justify buying the book.

9. **10 Natural Laws of Successful Time and Life Management: Proven Strategies for Increased Productivity and Inner Peace** by Hyrum W. Smith. Warner Books, January 1995, 240 pgs, paperback (34 reviews, 4.4 stars).

Note: The author's company, Franklin Quest, bought the Covey Leadership Center. The company was renamed FranklinCovey Co. in 1998. Smith and Covey are vice chairmen of the new company, which sells personal effectiveness products and training.

Upside — Reviewers liked the plainly written, conversational tone of the book. Many found it similar to books by Covey and Anthony Robbins but more practical. Several recommended using the book with the Franklin Planner.

Downside — A few said the system described was mainly for business executives. Some found Smith's success stories unrealistic and "sappy." Others didn't like the book's underlying religious agenda and the pitches for the Franklin Planner.

Our Take — A generally well-written book with an organized flow. While the book does have a Christian overtone (Smith, like Covey, is Mormon), the time management system is very good. Two-thirds of the book focuses on using the Franklin Planner. The last third, working with beliefs, rests on less secure conceptual footing. The final chapters on self-esteem, abundance mentality, and servant leadership are a bit preachy. Several illustrative stories are either dated or now disturbingly inappropriate (e.g., references to the World Trade Center). Some resources are no longer available. Still you may find the book helpful.

Note: You don't need this book to master the FranklinCovey planner. Find out more online, in a catalog, or at a FranklinCovey retail store (see Technique #5 — Use a Personal Planning System).

10. **Getting Things Done: The Art of Stress-Free Productivity** by David Allen. Penguin USA, January 2003, 288 pgs, paperback. 207 reviews, 4.5 stars).

Upside — Reviewers liked this book's practical, action-oriented advice. They said Allen's comprehensive, flexible system works well personally and professionally. Many who had tried other systems unsuccessfully liked this one. Several reviewers also recommended Allen's web site at *www.DavidCo.com*.

Downside — Some said the writing was abstract, theoretical, and wordy. A few thought the book was dry, repetitive, and too long. Some didn't like the business jargon. One reviewer skipped the 80-page introduction and still successfully implemented Allen's system.

Another rated the book lower because of its poor physical quality — flimsy cover; thin paper; and dim, small print.

Our Take — We agree with the downside reviewers. While people may like Allen's organization system, it's hard and time-consuming to implement. In addition, the book is rife with confusing detail and half-baked psychological theories. But hey, if it gets you organized and managing your life better, go for it.

11. **Time Tactics of Very Successful People** by B. Eugene Griessman. McGraw-Hill/Contemporary Books, June 1994, 240 pgs, paperback (20 reviews, 4.6 stars).

Upside — Reviewers thought the book was well written and to the point. They said it covered its topic very well and applied to both professional and personal situations. They thought ideas presented were functional and easily implemented.

Downside — Some reviewers felt the snippets-of-information format didn't give the book enough coherence. Others didn't like the contradictory tactics.

Our Take — We agree with the reviewers. The book is filled with excellent information. It's well written with appealing stories but is intentionally not an integrated system of time management. We found it a slow read. Most of the information on computers is dated. You'll like the book if you already manage time well. It's a good companion to any of the books at the top of this list.

12. **Making Work Work: New Strategies for Surviving and Thriving at the Office** by Julie Morgenstern. Fireside, September 2004, 272 pages, hardcover (9 reviews, 4.5 stars).

Upside — Reviewers said the book was helpful. One thought the ideas were original and insightful.

Downside — One reviewer said the book layout seemed crowded. Another said the book seemed oriented to females, although he found it applied to males as well. A third was angry that she'd been duped into buying the book, thinking it was new, not a rehash of one she'd bought before.

Our Take — The book presents nine competencies and 34 strategies on improving your productivity and your relationship to your job. Part of the book is repackaged information from the author's earlier books (#16 and #17 reviewed below). Like the author's other books, this one also suffers from too much analysis and pseudo-psychology and too many words. If you like lots of questionnaires and advice, you might find it helpful.

13. **Organized for Success: Top Executives and CEOs Reveal the Organizing Principles That Helped Them Reach the Top** by Stephanie Winston. Crown Business, August 2004, 256 pgs, hardback (10 reviews, 4.0 stars).

Upside — Many reviewers said they were inspired to pick up practical hints. Some said they loved all Winston's books. Several enjoyed peeking into the world of CEOs.

Downside — Some reviewers thought the book was disappointing, offering nothing new. Some thought the focus on CEOs wasn't helpful for everyone else.

Our Take — We concur with the reviewers. Winston has published previous books on getting organized. This one has a variety of strategies CEOs use to stay productive, some surprisingly counterintuitive and simple. The book isn't a system, so you have to poke around and put things together yourself. Good writing but a bit wordy.

14. **The Now Habit: A Strategic Program for Overcoming Procrastination and Enjoying Guilt-Free Play** by Neil A. Fiore. J. P. Tarcher, January 1989, 224 pgs, paperback (58 reviews, 4.6 stars).

Upside — Reviewers found this a practical read and liked the gentle, compassionate tone. They thought the book did a good job of covering the why's of procrastination. Some who'd been stuck for years said the book really helped them. Reviewers especially liked the idea of scheduling playtime first.

Downside — Some said the book was uninspiring, poorly designed, and stylistically flawed. Others thought it presented too much theory and not enough practice.

Our Take — We agree with the downside reviewers. The Now Habit program isn't clearly spelled out. There's too much psychological analysis. Long stories often don't forward the action. The chapter on self-talk is good but might not justify buying the book.

15. **First Things First: To Live, to Love, to Learn, to Leave a Legacy** by Stephen R. Covey, A. Roger Merrill, and Rebecca Merrill. Fireside/Simon & Schuster, reprint edition, January 1996, 373 pgs, paperback (57 reviews, 4.4 stars).

Upside – Reviewers thought the book was inspirational, a good companion to *The 7 Habits of Highly Effective People,* and a good primer for the FranklinCovey time management system. Most thought the book helped put principle-centered living effectively into action. Many appreciated learning how to get in touch with what matters most in their life. Several especially liked the process for writing a one-page mission statement (Appendix A).

Downside – Some thought the book was a rehash of *7 Habits.* Others said it was too long. Descriptions of the writing style were "overblown" and "disorienting," the latter referring to the way the book jumps from "we" to a specific author to segments by acquaintances of the authors. Some were put off by too much jargon, too many diagrams, complex concepts, and overuse of the word "paradigm." Others thought talking about leaving a legacy was off the mark for the book's primary audience — people who haven't made much money yet.

Our Take – We agree with the reviewers. This is not a basic time management book. It's too long, repetitive, and does rehash the *7 Habits* book. The chapter on Urgency Addiction is helpful; we summarize it under Technique #8 — Prioritize.

16. **Organizing from the Inside Out** by Julie Morgenstern. Owl Books, 1st edition, September 1998, 262 pgs, paperback (138 reviews, 4.4 stars).

    Upside — Most reviewers appreciated Morgenstern's simple, effective organizing system. Many especially liked learning why they are disorganized and being able to tailor recommendations to their own situations. They also liked the friendly writing style and felt the author understood them.

    Downside — Some reviewers felt the advice was too general, repetitious, and common sense. Others thought implementing the method took too much time and money (buying all those containers). Still others didn't like the writing and pseudo-psychology. Several reviewers commented on the book's small type. One felt duped because he/she had bought the book based on all the superlative reviews and then disliked it after reading it.

    Our Take — This a useful book — and the pseudo-psychology, repetition, and small type are annoying.

17. **Time Management from the Inside Out: The Foolproof System for Taking Control of Your Schedule and Your Life** by Julie Morgenstern. Henry Holt & Company, Inc., 1st edition, September 2000 and 2nd edition, September 2004, 288 pgs, paperback (35 reviews, 4.2 stars).

    Upside — A number of reviewers thought the book offered practical advice on understanding and managing time. Several liked the presentation of time as a tangible container. Others appreciated not having to swallow a one-size-fits all methodology.

    Downside — Some found the writing confusing, repetitive, boring, with too many rules and lists. Others disliked the self-help tone. Many said they preferred the author's book on organizing (#16).

    Our Take — We agree with the reviewers. The 2nd edition isn't significantly different from the 1st. Both books are uneven. Some parts are clear and useful. Others are confusing and unnecessarily complicated. The writing has a slightly patronizing, let-me-hold-your-hand tone. We don't think Morgenstern's system for organizing clutter works as well for managing time.

18. **Eat That Frog! 21 Great Ways to Stop Procrastinating and Get More Done in Less Time** by Brian Tracy. Berrett-Koehler Publishers, April 2001, 125 pgs, paperback (66 reviews, 4.1 stars).

Upside — Most reviewers said this was a short, easy read. They thought it was concise and clearly written. Many liked Tracy's simple principles and found the book a good reference on how to get into and stay in action. Many liked Tracy's metaphor of eating your ugliest frogs each day (your biggest, most important tasks).

Downside — Some reviewers didn't like the frog metaphor. Others thought the book was repetitive, somewhat condescending, and offered common sense solutions rather than new insights. Some found it a rehash of Tracy's other books. One person thought it was too heavy on self-discipline and too light on inspiration.

Our Take — The book is a list of "shoulds" and "musts" you've probably heard before. Tracy's advice is not only simple, it's simplistic. Most of his suggestions sound deceptively easy. However, using even half of them effectively requires a high degree of self-discipline, self-control, and willpower. If beating the procrastination out of yourself is not your cup of tea, skip this one.

19. **Following Through: A Revolutionary New Model for Finishing Whatever You Start** by Steve Levinson & Pete Greider. Kensington Publishing Corporation, October 1998, paperback. (22 reviews, 4.0 stars)

Upside — Reviewers liked the useful tactics for overcoming procrastination. Some thought the authors communicated their message clearly.

Downside — Several reviewers found the writing obtuse and shallow. Many complained that the model came too late in the book and was confusing. Some were disappointed there was no information on why they procrastinate. Others questioned the book's underlying evolutionary theory.

Our Take — We agree with the downside reviewers. The book lacks a clear, compelling structure. The writing is choppy and padded with long, meandering stories. The model of how we use our minds is unnecessarily complicated. Many positive reviews are anonymous, a sure sign that friends and relatives were trying to stack the deck in favor of the book.

20. **The Complete Idiot's Guide to Managing Your Time** by Jeffrey Davidson & Bob Losure. MacMillan Publishing, 3rd Edition, December 2001, 360 pgs, paperback (12 reviews, 4.3 stars).

Upside — Reviewers liked the short chapters and easy writing. They found it down-to-earth, relevant, and full of useful recommendations.

Downside — Some found the book thin on practical strategies for organizing work and time. One said the book was more appropriate for Americans than for people in other countries. Some didn't like the simplistic fixes for finding life meaning and balance.

Our Take — The book presents an overwhelming amount of information on a much broader range of topics than most time management books cover. The layout is distracting with too many headings, subheadings, and call-outs. The nuggets are there if you're patient in digging them out. Good editing could have cut 100 pages and made the book much stronger.

Note: We DO NOT RECOMMEND **Time Management for Dummies** by Jeffrey Mayer. Hungry Minds, Inc., 2nd Edition, May 1999, 408 pgs, paperback (13 reviews, 2.8 stars).

Downside — Most reviewers thought the book was more about sales techniques than time management. Many said the author plugged electronic products too much.

Appendix B

OTHER RECOMMENDED BOOKS

THESE BOOKS DIDN'T MAKE our annotated list because they don't deal directly with the specifics of time management. However, they can help you lead a happier, more fulfilled life.

The number of Amazon reviews is listed. All books were rated predominantly 5 stars.

Two books that challenge our obsession with speed and overwork:

- **Take Back Your Time: Fighting Overwork and Time Poverty in America** by John De Graaf. Berrett-Koehler Publishers, July 2003, 250 pgs, paperback (10 reviews).

- **In Praise of Slowness: How a Worldwide Movement is Challenging the Cult of Speed** by Carl Honore. Harper/ Collins, April 2004, 320 pgs, hardback (5 reviews).

Classic books on being more effective and productive:

- **The Seven Habits of Highly Effective People: Restoring the Character Ethic** by Stephen R. Covey. Fireside/Simon & Schuster, 1st Edition, September 1990; Free Press, 15th Anniversary Edition, November 2004, 384 pgs, paperback (576 reviews).

- **How to Win Friends and Influence People** by Dale Carnegie. Pocket Books, first published in 1936. Reissue edition February 1990, 304 pgs, paperback (359 reviews).

- **Think and Grow Rich** by Napoleon Hill. Ballantine Books, First published in 1937. Reissue edition November 1990, 256 pgs, paperback (248 reviews).

- **Influence: The Psychology of Persuasion** by Robert Cialdini. Perennial Currents, Revised Edition, October 1998, 336 pgs, paperback (133 reviews).

Three first-rate books on high performance:

- **How the Way We Talk Can Change the Way We Work: Seven Languages for Transformation** by Robert Kegan and Lisa Lahey. Jossey-Bass Publishers, December 2002, 256 pgs, paperback (5 reviews).

- **Play to Win: Choosing Growth Over Fear in Work and Life** by Larry Wilson and Hersch Wilson. Bard Press, Revised Edition, September 2004, 251 pgs, paperback (16 reviews).

- **The Power of Full Engagement: Managing Energy, Not Time, is the Key to High Performance and Personal Renewal** by Jim Loehr and Tony Schwarz. Free Press, hardcover, February 2003; 256 pgs, paperback, January 2005 (57 reviews).

Frequently recommended in Amazon reviews of other books:

- **Optimal Thinking: How to Be Your Best Self** by Rosalene Glickman. Wiley, March 2002, 256 pgs, paperback (63 reviews).

Two of our favorites on living an enlightened life:

- **The Power of Now: A Guide to Spiritual Enlightenment** by Eckhart Tolle. New World Library, October 1999, 224 pgs, paperback (462 reviews).

- **Siddhartha** by Herman Hesse, First published in German in 1922 and in English in 1951. Bantam Classic and Loveswept, January 1996 (others available), 160 pgs, paperback (347 reviews).

A quick, profound little read:

- **The Why You Are Here Café** by John Strelechy. Aspen Light Publishing, September 2003, 161 pgs, paperback (12 reviews).

Appendix C

HOW TO BUY BOOKS FOR (MUCH) LESS

1. *If you know a book's title*, first read the customer reviews of the book at ***www.Amazon.com***. There should be at least 5 reviews.

    DON'T BUY THE BOOK:

    *   If the reviews are not generally favorable. Trust your gut to weed out the unfair rants from the honest appraisals.

    *   If there are fewer than 5 reviews and the book is not newly published.

2. If the reviews are good or you want the book anyway, don't immediately buy it from Amazon. It may not be the cheapest place to get it (although often it is).

3. Go to ***www.BestBookBuys.com***. (Another URL for the site is ***www.BestWebBuys.com***.) Search on the book's title.

4. You'll get a list of books with any words in the title in bestselling order. Scroll to the one you want. You can also sort alphabetically or by date of publication.

Note: Look at titles closely; many books by different authors have similar or even the same titles. Also check the format since many books are available more than one way (e.g., hardcover, paperback, digital, CD, and cassette).

5. Click on either the hyperlinked title or the Compare Prices button for the book you want. You'll get a comparison chart of online bookstores selling the book, from lowest to highest price.

6. Click on Buy next to the bookstore name. You'll go directly to the online store's purchase page for that specific book. You haven't bought the book until you go through the store's ordering process.

7. *If you don't know a book's title,* you can also search at BestBookBuys by author, subject, keyword, or ISBN. ISBN of course turns up one specific book. You'll get a list if you search by author, subject, or keyword (keywords typically produce the longest lists). After you've found the book you want, follow the same process: Go to Amazon to read reviews, go back to BestBookBuys to Compare Prices, and Buy.

Current online bookstores offering the best prices and customer service (in alphabetical order):

- A1Books (and A1Textbooks)

- Amazon

- Buy

- Half (an eBay company)

- Overstock

- TextbookX

- Wal-Mart

Note: We DO NOT RECOMMEND buying cheap books from the main eBay website right now. The eBay auction process makes finding and buying books confusing and slow.

Can't find a book at the usual outlets? Search for it at these sites:

- *www.BookFinder.com*

- *www.BookSearch.com*

- *www.BiblioFind.com*

Appendix D

ABOUT THE AUTHORS

PAMELA DODD

Pam has focused on the dynamics of work groups and personal and organizational effectiveness for over 20 years. Client industries include energy, healthcare, manufacturing, and professional services. For seven years she worked for Electronic Data Systems, designing and delivering programs on diversity and leadership development. She has written about learning organizations for the American Society for Training and Development and edited the monograph *Pushing the Boundaries: Learning Organization Lessons from the Field*.

Pam has a B.A. in personnel administration from the University of Pennsylvania, a master's degree in social work from Marywood University, and a Ph.D. in organizational psychology and social work from the University of Michigan. She is a member of the American Psychological Association, the Association for Psychological Science, and the American Sociological Association.

DOUG SUNDHEIM

Doug is an organizational development consultant and executive coach. He frequently speaks on business and organizational topics to corporations and associations.

Selected clients include executives and managers from Altria Group Inc., Bertelsmann, The Chubb Corporation, DC Comics, DoubleClick, Prudential Douglas Elliman, Harvard Management Company, HSBC Bank USA, International Baccalaureate Organization, MetLife, and the University of Chicago.

Doug has a B.S. in psychology from Cornell University and 12 years' experience as a sales and business development manager, primarily in telecommunications and Internet consulting.

If you would like to order 10 or more copies of
The Best Time Management Tools & Techniques,
contact the publisher:

Peak Performance Press, Inc.
2232 South Main St., #476
Ann Arbor, MI 48103
(800) 344-5417